THE ANATOMY OF SAIL

THE YACHT DISSECTED AND EXPLAINED

Published by Adlard Coles Nautical
an imprint of
Bloomsbury Publishing Plc
50 Bedford Square,
London WC1B 3DP
www.adlardcoles.com

First edition published 2014

10 9 8 7 6 5 4 3 2 1

Hardback: 978-1-4729-0275-7
ePub: 978-1-4729-0924-4
ePDF: 978-1-4729-0925-1

A CIP catalogue record for this book is
available from the British Library.

This book is produced using paper
that is made from wood grown in
managed, sustainable forests. It is
natural, renewable and recyclable.
The logging and manufacturing
processes conform to the
environmental regulations of the
country of origin.

ART EDITOR: Louise Turpin
PHOTOGRAPHY: Nic Compton
and Joe McCarthy
Chapter 2 opener photograph
(p24–25) © Christian Février /
Bluegreen Pictures

Typeset in 10pt Avenir
Printed and bound in China by
Toppan Leefung Printing

Note: while all reasonable care
has been taken in the publication
of this book, the publisher takes
no responsibility for the use of the
methods or products described in
the book.

NIC COMPTON

THE ANATOMY OF SAIL

THE YACHT DISSECTED AND EXPLAINED

ADLARD COLES NAUTICAL

B L O O M S B U R Y

LONDON · NEW DELHI · NEW YORK · SYDNEY

Contents

INTRODUCTION

YOU MIGHT THINK YOU'VE PICKED UP A LOVELY PHOTOGRAPHIC BOOK CELEBRATING THE MOST BEAUTIFUL MODERN AND CLASSIC BOATS AROUND THE WORLD. AND SO YOU HAVE. ONLY WE'VE TRIED TO MAKE THIS ONE A LITTLE BIT DIFFERENT. RATHER THAN SIMPLY FILLING PAGE AFTER PAGE WITH PRETTY PICTURES, WE'VE ZOOMED IN REALLY CLOSE TO EXAMINE THE PHYSIOLOGY OF WHAT THOSE PICTURES ACTUALLY CONTAIN.

That wide angle action shot of the 1888 cutter *Partridge* storming down the Solent after her landmark restoration (p76)? Even a complete landlubber can sense the drama and respond to the picture on a compositional level. A boating geek, however, will be more interested in the complicated rigging arrangement and specialised hardware which the picture displays with anatomical precision. Likewise the shot of the Grand Surprise being craned out of the water in St Valery de Cau, with the picturesque terraced buildings of the old town behind (p36). The non-initiated might wonder how that boat is standing there, apparently balanced on nothing more than its narrow keel. Most experienced sailors will instantly recognise a modern racing design with an extreme hull form and want to know more.

Most sailing pictures can be read on two levels. We are surrounded by great images of boats which could yield valuable information not just about those particular vessels but about sailing boats in general, if only someone could 'interpret' the picture for us. Which is exactly what this book tries to do.

Opening with a general introduction to sailing, from its origins right up to the present, the book looks at the function of sailing boats and the materials from which they are made, as well as the major rig types. Chapter 2 looks at the main elements which make a boat – the bits that determine its visual character and behaviour under sail. This is all about form. Why do some boats have pointy bows while others have blunt bows? Which is safer at sea: the classic counter stern or the modern 'sugar scoop' stern? And why does that Grand Surprise have such a bloomin' deep keel?

Having discussed the general vocabulary of sailing, we then delve a bit deeper. Much deeper in fact. Chapters 3–7 examine specific parts of the sailboat's anatomy – the rig, deck structures, general hardware, accommodation and mechanics – and dissects them piece by piece to see what they do and how they differ from one boat to the next. There are countless types of cleats, for instance, so what makes one better for a particular job than another? Can you tell a symmetric spinnaker from an asymmetric one? A tri-radial from a cross-cut? And what, exactly, are mast spreaders for?

Along the way, the novice sailor will pick up all kinds of nautical jargon simply by looking at the many variations on a theme, while the more experienced might learn a thing or two as well (do you really know what a whisker is? Or when the first fin-keeled boat was designed? And what about Kelvin's balls?). Where necessary, diagrams are included for clarification and, for anyone who's new to all this, there's a crib sheet at the back in the form of a glossary.

Why collect all these photographs in the first place? My own obsession with boat gear no doubt stems from my childhood on boats, when my weekly job was to polish the brass. As well as door handles and latches, that included the steering wheel boss and rim, various rubbing strips and, if I was feeling brave, the drum on the aft windlass. In the evenings, I spent a lot of time lying in my bunk, counting the deck beams with my toes, which taught me all about the structural properties of a well-found wooden yacht.

Things got worse when I became a boatbuilder and was immersed in the minutiae of fitting out and repairing boats of various types, including wood, steel, glassfibre and ferrocement. There's nothing like being asked to shape a set of spars for a 50ft ketch from Douglas fir tree trunks to make you appreciate the correct dimensions of a wooden mast. Even when I turned to writing and photography and was sent on assignment to the Côte d'Azur, I couldn't stop myself taking as many pictures of cast bronze deck fittings and steamed mast hoops as of boats sailing across sparkling blue seas. Over the years, this addiction turned into a library of pictures, which in turn formed the basis of this book.

If I was just a photographer, no doubt I would have turned it all into a regular book of pretty pictures, but as a writer/photographer/sailor, I feel a duty to inform as well as to entertain. Hopefully this book achieves both those objectives.

1 THE BASICS

How were sailing boats created, and why? It's easy to take the modern pleasure yacht for granted, but for hundreds of years the primary purpose of sail was to power the working boats that fished, fought or ferried cargo and passengers around the world. Sailing for pleasure is a relatively recent phenomenon. And while most modern boats are made from fibreglass, there are many other materials that serve the purpose as well if not better, including wood, steel and concrete. This chapter looks at the functions sailboats serve, the materials from which they are made, and the most common types of rigs found on the water today.

WORKING BOATS

Ever since the first sailboat was invented in Mesopotamia more than 5,000 years ago, the majority of boats have been built to work. Trade was usually the driving force, as well as fishing and transport. Ancient Greece was largely built on the ability of ships to conquer foreign lands and maintain trade, as were the Roman, British and Spanish empires. Much of the world once depended on the cod caught by wooden fishing boats in the North Atlantic.

Workboats, then, have changed the course of human history. Yet, remarkably, no two workboat types are the same. Local geography, weather and materials have determined the shape and size of craft best suited to each particular area: massive barges to carry loads up and down the Thames; delicate catamarans to skip from island to island in the Pacific; seaworthy double-enders to negotiate the choppy seas off Norway; voluminous junks to carry loads up and down the Chinese coast, and so on.

Nowadays, motor boats have taken over the functions that sailing workboats used to fulfil in most parts of the world – with the notable exception of the Falmouth oyster boats, which still fish on the River Fal in

Cornwall in the old way, thanks to a bylaw designed to preserve the stock

of oysters. But the influence of working boats lives on, either directly in

boats converted to other uses, such as tourism, or indirectly in the design

aesthetic of contemporary designs – such as the Dutch botter, still built to

the same principles as working boats of 200 years ago.

CLOCKWISE FROM BOTTOM LEFT:
Sailing boats are still used to fish for
oysters on the River Fal.
Ireland's Hookers evolved as hardy, yet
beautiful, cargo carriers.
On the East Coast of America, schooners
such as the Mercantile carried cargo.
Thames barges were designed to carry
large loads around the coast of England.

RACING YACHTS

Cleopatra apparently liked nothing better than to cruise down the Nile on her own barge, and the Roman emperor Caligula built floating palaces to potter about Lake Nemi – so they were arguably the first yachtsman and yachtswoman. Sailing for pleasure didn't really take off until the 17th century, however, when the first *jaght* were launched in the Netherlands. Designed for speed rather than weight-carrying, these shallow, flat-bottomed craft were used to carry pilots to waiting ships or to chase pirates and smugglers. They soon caught the eye of wealthy traders who decided to have some built for their own fun – and thus the sport of yachting was born.

Yacht design has evolved dramatically in the 400 years since then, with the prevailing 'cod's head and mackerel tail' (ie bluff bow and slender stern) giving way to almost exactly the opposite approach. Today's ocean racers have fine bows to cut through the water, with wide, flat sterns to surf down the waves. Instead of long keels running the whole length of the boat, they have narrow fins with great lozenges of lead hanging down deep below the hull. And, instead of squat, low canvas sails, they have tall, narrow fingers of Kevlar reaching up into the sky.

RIGHT: The famous J-Class yachts were used to race for the America's Cup in the 1930s. After more than 50 years' absence, they are now back in fashion among the super-rich.

BOTTOM, LEFT TO RIGHT: The selection series for the 2013 America's Cup was raced on 42ft (13m) catamarans, before switching to 72-footers (22m) for the actual Cup.
A modern racing fleet makes an early start for the Round the Island race off Cowes, in the UK.
The America's Cup Class was used to race for the Cup from 1992 to 2007.

CRUISING YACHTS

For the first 200 years, yachting was mainly about racing. People who went 'cruising' in the current sense of the word were called explorers, and indeed the ship which first discovered Australia for the Europeans was a Dutch *jaght* by the name of *Duyfken*. It wasn't until the late 18th century that the idea of sailing long distances for pleasure began to gain credence. Robert Louis Stevenson was one of the first cruising yachtsmen, and in 1888 chartered a yacht to sail across the Pacific. He was followed a few years later by Joshua Slocum, who in 1898 became the first man to sail around the world single-handed. It took him more than three years – a leisurely cruise indeed, compared to the current record of under two months for the same journey.

A successful cruising yacht combines spacious accommodation with ease of handling, a comfortable motion at sea, and hopefully good looks. At the same time, no one wants to sail a slouch, and sailing just one knot (ie one mile per hour) slower can add up to several days' delay when crossing oceans. A successful design is a compromise between comfort and speed – which to a modern mind suggests a long fin keel, which gives good speed while making the boat docile to handle and shallow enough to explore remote anchorages.

TOP: The Victoire 37 is a contemporary cruising yacht built in Holland with a traditional appearance, but a modern fin keel and full amenities.

ABOVE: Catamarans, such as this 62ft (19m) Tribe, can make comfortable and stable cruising yachts. They are also fast, reaching speeds of up to 35 knots.

OPPOSITE PAGE, TOP: The Sunsail F40 is a 'performance cruiser' developed by the charter company Sunsail. Although aimed at beginners, these boats still require a competent skipper and crew.

BOTTOM: A traditional cruising yacht with a long keel provides a steady ride, if not a very exciting one. The 1957 Caper is fitted with a modern rig on a classic hull, making her easier to handle.

RIG TYPES

Sedans, coupés, hatchbacks, estates, sports, pick-ups, 4 x 4, SUVs, campers… Just as cars come in many shapes and sizes, so do sailing boats, and it takes a bit of practice to recognise them. Like car engines, different sail plans serve different purposes. One is powerful but tricky to handle (eg lugger), while another is more versatile (eg gaff cutter), and another more suited to short-handed sailing (eg ketch).

New materials and equipment also play a major role in the development of sails. It's long been known that a single large sail is more efficient than several small sails, for instance, which is why cutters and sloops are the rigs of choice for racing. Until the invention of winches, however, all that sail area had to be controlled by hand using blocks and many, many yards of rope. It's no coincidence that the largest cutter ever built (the 1903 America's Cup defender *Reliance*) also sported the first ever set of underdeck winches. Even with the benefit of winches, large sails need large crews to handle them, which is why sail plans with two masts, such as ketch or yawl, are preferred by cruising folk, who are more interested in comfort than speed.

Logic aside, sailors often favour certain types of rig for purely aesthetic or cultural reasons – which is why Americans love schooners and Brits love cutters.

ABOVE: A full-rigged ship from the Age of Sail. The three forward masts carry square sails on their horizontal spars, or yards. This is the rig that powered famous ships such as the Cutty Sark.

OPPOSITE PAGE, CLOCKWISE FROM TOP LEFT: The gaff ketch rig is extremely versatile and ideal for this Norwegian rescue boat.
Fewer, bigger sails provide more power, however, which is why racing boats are usually rigged as sloops.
For long ocean crossings, the schooner rig is hard to beat, especially on a boat this size (the 181ft/51m Shenandoah).

BELOW: The lug rig is essentially a square sail turned sideways, with one end of the yard pushed out. It was widely used by fishing boats, such as this French replica.

WOOD

ABOVE: Built in 1973 from triple layers of laminated mahogany, Naif came at the end of the wooden boat era – after everyone had switched en masse to fibreglass.

BELOW: Traditional wooden boatbuilding at the International Yacht Restoration School (IYRS) in Newport, Rhode Island. This is a typical carvel planked hull, where the planks are fitted edge to edge. The large angular structures are the templates (or moulds) that are removed once the planking is complete.

Once upon a time, all boats were built of wood – be it dug-out canoes, balsa rafts or laboriously jointed Viking longboats. And wood is still the most versatile and easy to repair building material for yachts. Trouble is, it also tends to split, crack, rot and generally try by any means to turn itself back into vegetable matter. Modern materials, such as plywood and epoxy, have helped improve the durability of wooden boats, as well as making them easier to build. Whereas in the past you'd need a six-year apprenticeship to build a boat using traditional methods, nowadays anyone with basic skills and a little common sense can knock one up using the stitch and glue method. Even luxury superyachts are often built of wood, as modern strip-plank technology can be the most efficient way to build a large, one-off design.

Yacht builders have developed something of a bad name among environmentalists due to their extensive use of rainforest timbers such as teak and mahogany. Even though the total amount used by boatbuilders is relatively tiny compared to, say, furniture makers, it is nevertheless incumbent on all craftsmen to make sure all their timber comes from sustainable sources. One solution is to only use local timbers, such as oak, elm and larch, although these tend to be less durable than tropical timbers. Again, modern boatbuilding techniques mean that some timbers not commonly used for constructing yachts, such as cedar, can now be used with alacrity.

ABOVE: An exquisite sailing dinghy built using indigenous timbers at the Wooden Boat Centre in Tasmania. The hull is clinker-built, which means the edges of the planks overlap. The frames (transverse timbers) will be steamed in next.

BELOW: Wood is still used for large one-off projects, such as this 70ft (21m) cruising yacht. Narrow strips of wood (usually cedar) are glued edge to edge, and the hull is sealed with epoxy and sheathed below the waterline with a thin layer of fibreglass.

FIBREGLASS & COMPOSITE

When fibreglass first appeared in the 1960s, it was hailed as the ultimate boatbuilding material. Relatively cheap to build (once you had the mould), durable and requiring minimal maintenance, fibreglass yachts certainly seemed like the modern answer to those attention-seeking old wooden boats. And certainly the new medium helped democratise sailing, as the public reaped the benefits of standardisation in lower prices and predictable performance. Anyone could buy a 24ft yacht, stick it in a marina and not worry about whether the decks were going to dry out during a long hot summer or rot away during a long wet winter.

But the new medium wasn't quite as foolproof as originally thought. Like wood, it proved to be porous and if the lay up wasn't done correctly, water infiltrated the fibre and caused 'fibreglass pox', or osmosis, which was messy and expensive to treat. There was also the question of what to do with the boats once they were no longer needed, as unlike their wooden counterparts they were unlikely to just rot away. Since the 1990s, the technology has been improved to get rid of the problem of osmosis. The problem of what to do with the old ones remains, however, and the number of elderly fibreglass boats grows year by year.

OPPOSITE PAGE, TOP: This Class 40 racing boat is built out of 'infused' fibreglass to be as light as possible. The hull, deck and internal structures all have foam cores.

CENTRE LEFT: The mould of the Contessa 32 yacht built by Jeremy Rogers. The inside of this mould is lined with gel coat and fibreglass to create the boat's hull.

CENTRE RIGHT: The Folkboat is the quintessential affordable sailing boat, originally built in wood and now produced by the hundreds in fibreglass.

BOTTOM: Pop open the Contessa mould, and this is what you get: a sleek, safe and reliable cruising yacht that has a cult following around the world.

BELOW: The Tofinou 9.5 is a modern fibreglass boat with traditional styling. The deck is fibreglass too, but with an 8mm layer of teak to please the eyes and feet.

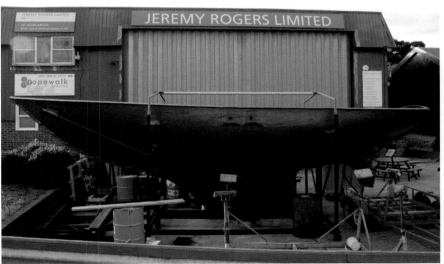

STEEL & FERRO

So what is the cheapest, strongest and most easily repaired boatbuilding material? By quite a long way, steel. Like plywood, steel holds a curve with little support, so minimal moulds or frames are needed to achieve the desired shape. Unlike plywood, it can be bent into a compound curve to create rounded topsides, although this is a rather specialised business and amateur builds tend to be built with the hard corners (or chines) that characterise plywood hulls. The finished hull will never leak (apart from where holes are cut for through-hull fittings), can bounce off a reef and suffer only minor scratches, and has excellent resale value.

So why aren't all boats made of steel? Good question. The main reason is that you can't mass produce hulls in steel like you can with fibreglass, which means construction is more specialised, which means the number of designs available is more limited. The other reason is that most sailors like to work on their boats themselves and, whereas everyone can have a bash with a hammer and chisel, not everyone can weld. Aluminium has all the advantages of steel with the added benefit of being 30% lighter but is difficult to weld, making it expensive to build commercially and putting it out of reach of the amateur builder.

TOP: It takes considerable skill to produce a hull this shape out of steel. The Dutch are past masters of the technique, however, and Windbreker was built by a professional shipbuilder in his spare time. Her liveaboard owners sailed her round Britain in 2013.

BOTTOM LEFT: The rows of rivets joining the steel plates are clearly visible on the hull of the Thames barge Portlight. The rivets may have failed on the Titanic when she hit the iceberg, but they've kept this old workhorse afloat for nearly 90 years.

BOTTOM CENTRE: Attaching fittings to a steel deck is easy: you just weld them in place. This cleat has been galvanised and finished off with a couple of teak rings bolted to the top of each bollard.

BOTTOM RIGHT: A boat made of cement? Will it float? Ferrocement is a much-maligned boatbuilding material, mainly due to poor amateur constructions. In the right hands, it can produce beautiful, long-lasting and maintenance-free hulls. And, because of its inherent strength, it can end up lighter than either wood or steel.

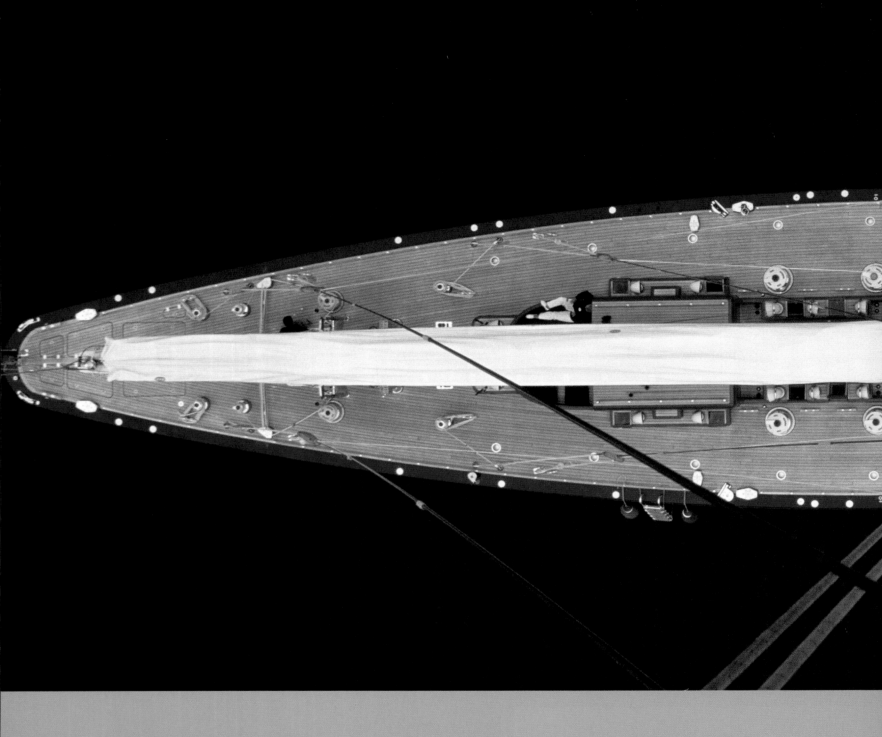

2 HULL & DECK

One of the delights of sailing is that, probably more than any other area of human activity, form follows function. The old saying that 'if it looks good, it will sail fast' still holds true – with a few notable exceptions. But what does a fine, overhanging bow tell us about a boat's performance under sail? How do the modern truncated sterns compare to the elegant counters of yesteryear? And what effect do the various keel and rudder arrangements have once a yacht heels to the breeze? This chapter explores the myriad of hull shapes that not only provide a visual feast for photographers but also define a yacht's character.

BOWS

Like the bonnet of a car, the bow of a boat has a disproportionate impact on its overall appearance. One glance at a long, overhanging bow immediately shouts 'classic!', while a stubby, upright stem suggests modern cruiser/racer. Of course, it's not quite that simple, and the Victorians were just as keen on upright (or 'plum') stems as the current round-the-cans racing types. Partly it's about racing rules; partly it's about fashion. Thus, when racing rules were based on waterline length, designers drew hulls with long overhangs, so that when the boat heeled over the effective waterline length became longer. And, generally, the longer the waterline length, the greater the speed. Most current racing rules measure a boat's total length, however, so the fad is for upright stems as there's no point in wasting boat length for the sake of a raked stem.

For cruising folk unaffected by such fads, the arguments are more about which shape is the most sea-kindly. There are those who argue that a well-raked bow reduces pitching (fore-and-aft motion). But again there are other factors to consider, such as the amount of flare in the bow, which increases buoyancy and also helps keep the crew dry. At the end of the day, cruising folk have to pay marina fees which are based on overall length. Every inch given over to a raked stem means an increase in berthing fees. Which is why the fashion for upright stems is becoming increasingly in evidence in cruising boats.

OPPOSITE PAGE: The bow (or stem) of the one-design Figaro (version 1) is angled forward to create a slight rake. This gives more buoyancy forward which results in a more sea-kindly motion.

TOP RIGHT: The clipper bow so beloved of American sailors – and the British prior to 1893.

CENTRE RIGHT: Brutal but effective: the vertical bow of the Volvo Open 70 maximises the boat's length.

BOTTOM RIGHT: The spoon bow became fashionable in the UK after the future King George V launched Britannia in 1893.

What a difference 114 years makes! When the 70ft cutter *Partridge* was built in Southampton in 1885, the era of so-called 'plank-on-edge' yachts was just coming to an end. Designed to take advantage of a racing rule which penalised beam but not draft, the boats of this period had extremely narrow and very deep hulls, with great clouds of sail balanced by many tons of lead bolted to the bottom of their keels. The result was a boat that heeled over in the slightest breeze and went through waves like a submarine. Although not as extreme as other yachts of this era, some of which were six times as long as they were wide, *Partridge*'s design was clearly influenced by the type.

By the time *Hugo Boss* was built in 1999, yacht design had been through every kind of permutation imaginable, but the general consensus was that wide boats were fast. This was particularly the case with a class known as the Open 60 ('open' because designers were free to innovate within certain parameters, and '60' because they were 60ft long) which dominated round-the-world races such as the Vendée Globe. Designed to surf down the waves of the Southern Ocean, they had wide, flat sterns – not unlike those of planing dinghies – and fine bows to cut through the waves. At their most extreme, their beam was almost a third of their length – the exact opposite principle from the 'plank on edge' yachts that dominated racing 114 years before.

At 68ft (21m) long, Partridge (LEFT) is almost half as wide as Hugo Boss (RIGHT), with a beam of 10ft 8in (3.2m) compared to the other's 18ft 2in (5.56m). Underwater, Partridge has a long keel which is more than 9ft (2.8m) deep, while the newer boat flattens out like a skimming dish – apart from her bulb keel which hangs an incredible 14ft 8in (4.5m) deep.

STERNS

As with bows, there are historic, practical and aesthetic reasons a yacht's stern is shaped the way it is. Historically, the same rules which encouraged long, overhanging bows did exactly the same for the other end. As the rules were based on waterline length, a yacht could have a long counter stern which measured nothing on the waterline when the boat was upright, but added several feet of 'free' waterline length once the boat was heeled. And as we've seen, a longer waterline equals greater speed. But racing rules don't explain why working boats such as Britain's legendary East Coast smacks have counter sterns to die for. Here, the reasons are probably more to do with the increased deck space and seaworthiness – a counter stern gives more buoyancy aft and is less likely to be 'pooped' by a following sea.

As with bows, once the rules focused on overall length, sterns became more upright to maximise the waterline length. Indeed, from the 1960s onwards, reverse transoms became fashionable as a means of reducing weight – although with the obvious disadvantage of reducing the space available for decks, cockpits, lockers and accommodation. That's less of an issue nowadays, with the enormously wide sterns prevalent on most modern yachts giving ample space for everything from boarding ladders to tenders, lifeboats and even the occasional jet ski!

1. Canoe sterns such as this are relatively unusual but produce elegant and seaworthy boats. Serenade is an N-Class yacht designed to America's Universal Rule.
2. At the other extreme is this reverse stern, which reduces weight aft while giving a longer waterline when the boat is heeled.
3. These elegant counter sterns are typical of the Dragon class, designed in 1929 – apart from Shamal, which is an Etchell class designed in 1967.
4. An elegant, almost heart-shaped, transom stern on the 1974 Italian yacht Chaplin.

5. The 'sugar scoop' stern of this modern cruising yacht makes a wonderful swimming platform, but offers less protection in a following sea.
6. Small transom sterns were in fashion in the 1970s.
7. A short counter stern with a small transom, courtesy of master designer William Fife, c.1897.
8. A reverse transom with a gate and a step to facilitate access.
9. The long counter stern on this 12-Metre is typical of yachts built to the International Rule of 1907–1939.

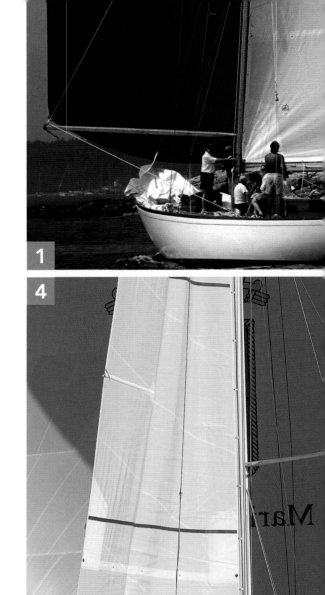

1

4

2

3

5

6

7

8

9

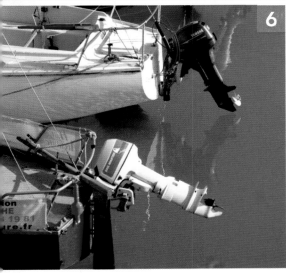

It doesn't get much more different than this. The flat, wide stern on the Open 60 *Hugo Boss* creates a huge cockpit with space for a dozen winches and jammers. It's ideal for surfing down those Southern Ocean waves, but it doesn't give much headroom down below – which is absolutely fine, considering most of the time it's sailed by one person, who pretty much lives in his or her control seat in the saloon. The stern is so buoyant, a large following sea can only lift it and drive it forwards in one long helter-skelter ride.

By contrast, the elegant counter on the 1897 cutter *Sayonara* sweeps up into a narrow aft deck, with a compact cockpit but plenty of length to take the sheets from the long, overhanging boom. There's not much space in the counter itself, apart from some storage in a small lazarette, but once you step down the hatch into the hull proper, there's ample headroom in her deep, narrow hull. The counter also gives her some reserve buoyancy, which means a big wave will lift the stern, rather than breaking over it.

BELOW: The 57ft (17m) cutter Sayonara was designed by William Fife and built in Adelaide in 1897. She proved invincible in racing on Port Phillip Bay.

RIGHT: Alex Thompson was sailing Hugo Boss singlehanded around the world in 2006 when he had to abandon her in the Southern Ocean as a result of keel damage.

SHEERS

ABOVE: The replica Victorian cutter Integrity fulfils the criteria of a classic-looking sheer, with the lowest point about 80-85% from the bow.

BELOW: Modern yachts sit higher in the water than traditional boats. A flat sheer, such as on this Bénéteau Océanis 50, helps reduce the boat's overall height and makes it appear more streamlined.

Drawing a fine bow and an elegant stern is all very well, but what about the bit in between – you know, the bit that makes up most of the boat? The line of a yacht, known as the sheer, is very rarely absolutely straight. Even when it appears to be straight, such as on some modern racing yachts, it's likely to have a slight concave to compensate for the optical illusion of the bow and stern appearing to droop slightly. Getting the curve exactly right so that it looks good not just when viewed straight from the side but from the bow and stern, high and low, and all angles in between is what separates the good from the excellent designer.

Traditionally, a yacht's stern is the same height as its middle point (ie amidships), while the lowest point is located 80–85% of the length from the bow. That means the line of the sheer keeps getting lower long after

passing the middle of the boat, and then rises up again fairly quickly at the stern. It's a formula that's produced many exceptionally beautiful yachts but which is rarely applied these days. Modern yachts are also likely to sit much higher out of the water (ie have more freeboard), thanks to their lighter displacement and more voluminous hulls, and a flat sheer line helps reduce the apparent height of the hull (freeboard).

35

TOP LEFT: The endlessly long sheer of a 6-Metre yacht. The photo shows how the overhangs lengthen the waterline when the boat is heeled over.

TOP RIGHT: The 1963 Strale has a reverse sheer (ie bow and stern droop down) and cutaway bow. Despite her racing success, her unusual looks never caught on.

BOTTOM: The jaunty sheer of the Maine windjammer Mercantile is exaggerated by her bowsprit. Most bowsprits are designed as a continuation of the line between the top of the stern and the top of the bow.

KEELS

For centuries, boats were all built with one type of keel: a long (or 'full') keel. The shape of the hull might vary – from a rounded canoe type to a wine glass shape and anything in between – but the keel always ran the entire length of the hull with the rudder attached to the back of it. The advantages of long keels are that they are simple to build and they steer in a straight line; the disadvantages are that they create a lot of wetted surface area (which creates unnecessary drag and therefore slows the boat down) and are tricky to manoeuvre.

The first designer to experiment with a fixed fin keel was the 'wizard of Bristol' Nat Herreshoff, who had some success with the idea back in the 1890s. Unfortunately, the concept was given a bad name by other designers who designed some very unseaworthy fin-keelers indeed, and the idea was abandoned for another 60 years or so. Then in the 1960s a series of designs featuring separate keels and rudder – including Olin Stephens's 1967 America's Cup defender *Intrepid* – achieved sensational results, trouncing all the long-keeled oldies in their path. Boat design would never be the same again. The advantages of fin keels are low wetted surface area (therefore less drag) and ease of manoeuvrability; the disadvantages are they are more 'nervy' to steer and get knocked about more in heavy weather.

Nowadays, practically all modern boats have fin keels, and the only question is how deep the fin should be. For cruising boats, most sailors prefer shallower keels, while for racing, ever-deeper keels with ever-heavier bulbs attached to the bottom are *de rigueur*.

TOP: This is the shape of an extreme racing yacht: the wide flat hull allows her to surf down the waves; the deep, narrow keel puts her ballast as low as possible. The Grand Surprise provides a fast but nervy ride.

BOTTOM LEFT: The opposite of the Grand Surprise's fin keel is a traditional long keel, such as on this small cruising yacht.

BOTTOM CENTRE: A centreboard is handy for exploring shallow waters, though it usually performs less well than a fixed keel.

BOTTOM RIGHT: With a deep fixed keel, this yacht was unable to move once she got stuck on rocks on a falling tide on the east coast of Ireland. She was refloated undamaged on the following tide.

RUDDERS

The shape of a boat's rudder is closely related to the type of keel it's got. A boat with a long keel will almost always have the rudder hung from the back of the keel – although its exact size and shape will vary from boat to boat. A rudder in this position has the advantage of being extremely well supported and protected from passing debris by the keel itself; but it has the disadvantage of requiring more effort to turn it, which is why wheels rather than tillers are usually installed on boats more than about 40ft (12.2m) long.

With the advent of fin keels in the 1960s, however, rudders acquired a life of their own. Henceforth, they would either be built as free-standing 'spade' rudders or hung on a 'skeg', a kind of fin attached to the bottom of a boat aft of the keel. The advantage of a spade rudder is that it can be 'balanced', making it easier to turn than a traditional rudder (see diagram) and making it more effective in reverse. The disadvantage is that in certain conditions it can 'stall' and become ineffective, leading to some exciting sailing. This, combined with the greater protection afforded by a skeg, is why most builders of cruising boats favour skeg-hung rudders.

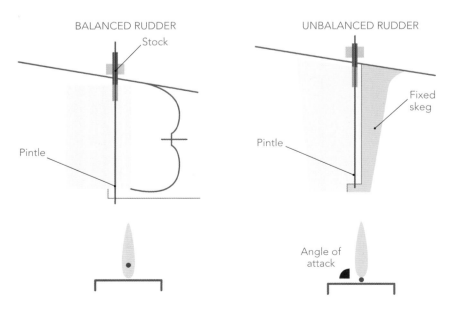

BALANCED VS UNBALANCED RUDDERS

By placing the leading edge of the rudder slightly ahead of the pivot point, the flow of water is used to help turn the helm.

BALANCED RUDDER

Stock

Pintle

UNBALANCED RUDDER

Fixed skeg

Pintle

Angle of attack

1. *As traditional as it gets: a stern-hung rudder on the Matthew replica, c.1497.*
2. *This America's Cup catamaran is fitted with a rudder on each hull.*
3. *A transom-hung rudder on a modern racing yacht.*
4. *The long keels on these traditional designs give maximum protection to the rudder.*
5. *This rudder is separate from the keel, but is supported by a fixed skeg.*
6. *A hinged rudder fitted to a small dinghy.*
7. *Many modern yachts have double rudders, which are more efficient when the boat is heeled over.*

ABOUT: *A non-slip surface can be applied to plywood decks using specialist paint.*

TOP LEFT: *A traditional, 'laid' deck, made of yellow Columbian pine. The lines of fastenings (sealed with wooden plugs) suggest this deck is solid. Note how the planks are parallel and 'nibbed' into the varnished 'margin' plank on either side.*

DECKS

Everyone loves a teak deck, which is why even some of the most innovative modern yachts, with composite hulls, carbon fibre masts and Spectra sails, still have teak decks. Not that those decks are 'real' wood. The vast majority of teak decks nowadays are actually composed of a ³/₈in (10mm) layer of teak stuck onto fibreglass or plywood. To some, this represents the best of both worlds: the undeniable beauty of a teak deck without the associated leaks and ongoing maintenance issues. To others it's a recipe for disaster, as water will inevitably find its way between the layers and cause irreparable damage.

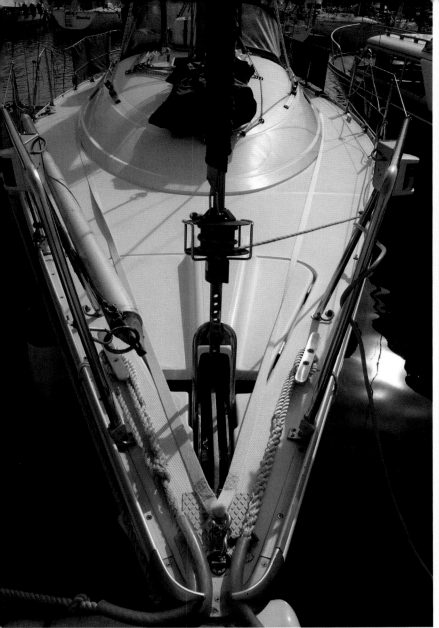

'Twas not always thus. In the old days, decks were either made of solid teak (for yachts) or pitch pine (for working boats) and sealed with tar. Laying a teak deck is an expensive and time-consuming business, however, so when smaller, more inexpensive yachts came on the market, these were invariably decked with tongue-and-groove planks covered in canvas, with a layer of white lead in between and paint mixed with sand on top (for grip). This lasted surprisingly well, although it has since been supplanted by the modern equivalent: plywood covered with fibreglass cloth, saturated with epoxy and painted over with purpose-made deck paint. Cheap and very, very effective.

OPPOSITE, RIGHT: A modern 'laid' deck, made of thin teak planks glued to a plywood subdeck. The lack of fastenings give the game away! Note how the planks are curved to the shape of the hull and 'nibbed' into the centre or 'king' plank.

ABOVE, LEFT: A modern deck and cabin is moulded in fibreglass as a single piece, and then attached to the hull. A non-slip surface can be built into the mould.

ABOVE, RIGHT: Plywood decks can also be sheathed in fibreglass to give a watertight covering. This is the modern version of tongue-and-groove decks covered with canvas and paint – only a lot more effective.

BULWARKS

Bulwarks are the little raised 'walls' which run around the edge of a boat's deck. They can be either an extension of the hull or attached separately to the deck. They are wonderful things as they stop objects rolling overboard, protect the decks and cabin trunk from the elements, act as a foot stop when the boat is heeled over, and generally give a feeling of security on deck. In fact, there are about 101 reasons why a yacht should have bulwarks and almost none why it shouldn't.

Yet, in spite of the many advantages of bulwarks, most modern yachts are built without them and are fitted instead with minimal toe rails, usually made out of pre-fabricated aluminium strips. This trend seems to be a hangover from racing, where crews sit on the windward rail with their legs hanging overboard to increase stability. In this scenario, a full-height bulwark would poke uncomfortably into their thighs. In practice, however, most boats are used for cruising where crews rarely sit with their legs over the side and where protection from the elements is of far greater importance. The only other area of debate is the question of aesthetics. Whereas a boat fitted with bulwarks looks delightfully salty and perhaps a tad old-fashioned, there is something undeniably cool and modern-looking about a boat with no bulwarks and just the raw join of deck to hull showing. But then surely no sailor would choose looks over safety?

TOP LEFT: When the going gets tough… a bulwark provides a useful bracing point on this 1897 classic yacht.

TOP RIGHT: The 1987 yacht Scarlet Oyster takes groups of young people racing as part of the Ellen MacArthur Cancer Trust's work. A low aluminium toe rail allows the crew to sit out to leeward comfortably.

BOTTOM LEFT: By the 1970's, fibreglass had taken over from wood, and deep bulwarks were replaced by low toerails – though sometimes still made of wood, such as on this 55ft Swan.

BOTTOM RIGHT: Assembling the bulwark on a wooden boat. The gap between the bulwark and the deck allows the water to flow straight off without the need for any scuppers.

FIGUREHEADS & CARVINGS

There's nothing so quintessentially salty as the prow of a ship with a figurehead tucked under the bowsprit. It goes hand-in-hand with gold earrings, bottles of rum and walking the plank in the common lexicon of ships. And there's little doubt that their use stretches back to at least Viking and Ancient Greek times. Studies show that figureheads were endowed with magical powers and were thought to protect a ship from enemies. Others suggest they are linked to the idea of a ship as a living creature and allowing it to 'see' the way ahead. Along with these theories there is the strong probability that sailors carved them just because they thought they looked pretty.

Whatever their origins, they certainly come in all shapes and sizes: birds, horses, dolphins, snakes, dragons and even, in post-Revolution France, a guillotine! Semi-clad women were a recurring theme among sailors who thought it was unlucky to have a woman aboard ship unless she was naked, in which case she calmed the seas. Lions were a favourite in 17th century Europe as a symbol of power, while the spread eagle has been popular in the USA since it was adopted as its national symbol in 1792. Popular figures such as Jean-Jacques Rousseau and various US presidents have been depicted, while shipowners weren't adverse to immortalising themselves as figureheads on their own ships.

ABOVE: Lions were a favourite motif in the 17th century, as symbols of power. This lion carved on the tiller of a Dutch barge looks quite meek, however.

OPPOSITE PAGE
1. *Fancy scrollwork on the bow of the replica classic yacht Sunshine, built in 2004.*
2. *Seabird is another replica of a William Fife yacht, with simple scrollwork on her clipper bow.*
3. *Snoopy is a genuinely old ship's tender dating from 1937 – though we suspect the carving on her stern is a more recent addition.*
4. *The frigate Shtandart was the original flagship of the Russian navy and was richly decorated with carvings – many of which were reproduced on the 1999 replica shown here.*
5. *The American eagle, as featured on the slave ship Amistad, and many other American boats besides.*
6. *Naked women are another recurrent theme, as on the 1902 schooner Shenandoah.*

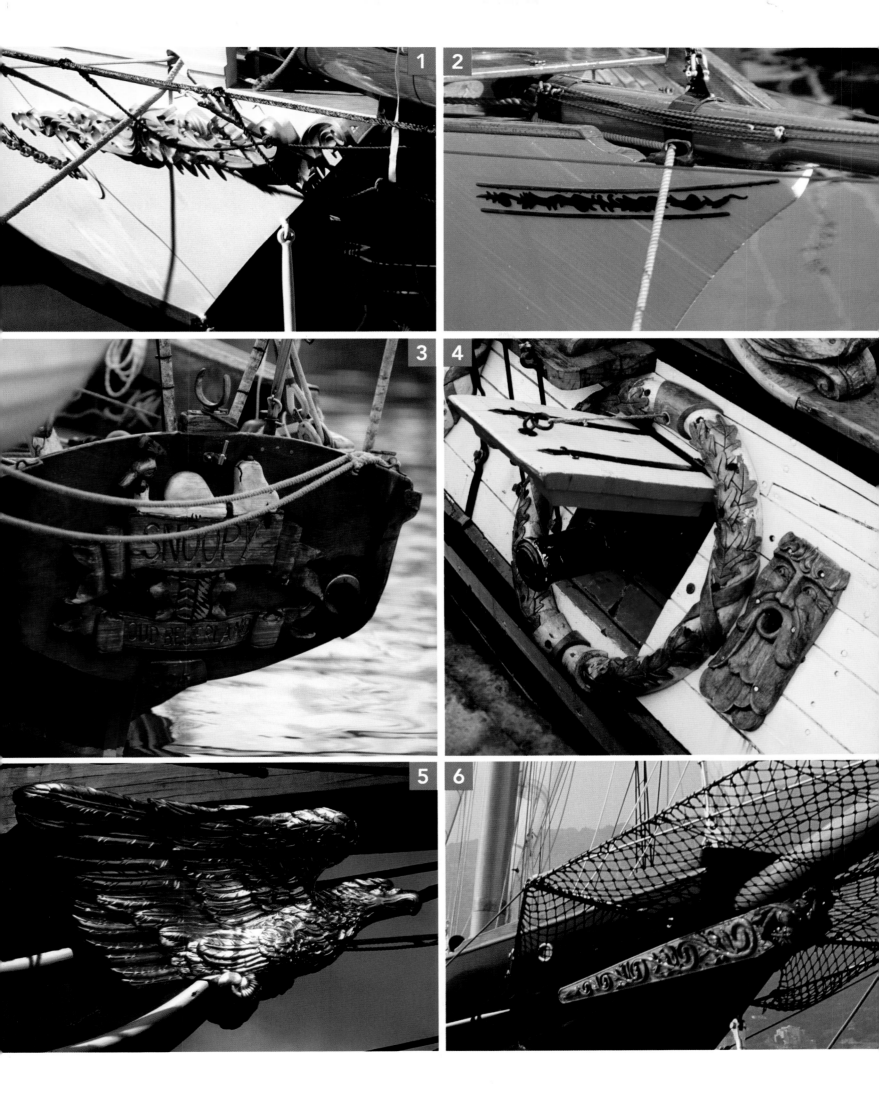

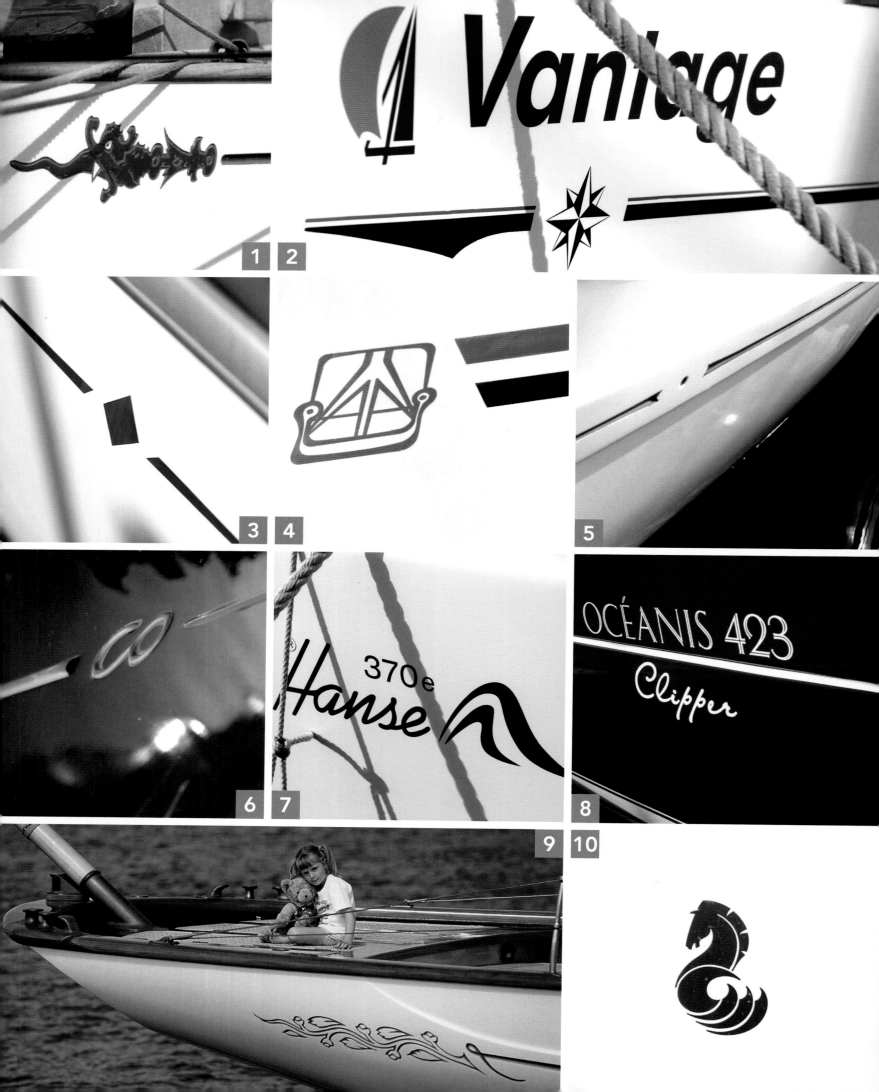

COVE LINES

OPPOSITE PAGE:
1. *The most famous brand in British yachting history: William Fife carved a dragon motif on the bows of all his boats from 1888 onwards.*
2. *The compass rose is the logo of the second biggest boatbuilder in the world: Jeanneau.*
3. *The Viking boat motif belongs to French boatbuilding company Dufour.*
4. *This was Bavaria's logo until about 2000, when it got a rebranding more in keeping with its luxury ethos.*
5. *A simple dot motif identifies this Cutlass 27.*
6. *The 'CO' stands for Contessa, an evergreen yacht from the 1970s, still in production.*
7. *Hanse is one of the biggest boatbuilders in the world.*
8. *At the other end of the Bénéteau cove line is the class (Océanis 423), and styling (Clipper).*
9. *At the other end of a Fife cove line is a pretty line of foliage.*
10. *The logo of the biggest boatbuilder in the world: Bénéteau.*

On cars, they're known as 'go faster' stripes, while on yachts they're given the more elegant name of cove lines, or even cavita lines. Whatever the name, the effect of a long line along the side of a car or boat is the same: to make the object look longer and more streamlined. A single gold line no more than ¾in (18mm) wide was deemed sufficient on most classic sailing yachts while modern boats, with their barn door topsides, often need two or more wide bands to give them a semblance of sleekness.

Cove lines are often combined with the maker's logo to create a distinctive company style, and most of the big names such as Bénéteau, Bavaria and Jeanneau have used them to good effect. The most famous image of all, however, is the fancy gold dragon used by the legendary Scottish yacht designer William Fife III. He is thought to have adopted the symbol after the success of his 1888 design *Dragon* and to have carved it on every boat built at his yard in Fairlie thereafter – although no two are exactly the same. Nowadays, his designs are the most sought-after yachts in the world, and a genuine Fife dragon carved in the bow of any boat will automatically double or even treble its value.

RIGHT: *No two Fife dragons are the same, which suggests a fun game of spot-the-boat. This one belongs to the 1911 racing yacht Tonino, originally owned by King Alfonso XIII of Spain. Can you guess the name of the boat in Picture 1? (Answer on p192)*

CHAPTER

3 RIG

They say that if two boats meet on the water, it's called a race. And there is an innate competitive streak in most sailors that means they will tweak, tug and tease a boat's sails until it's going as fast as they can make it go. That happens even if there isn't another boat to race against, and is magnified tenfold for every other boat on the horizon. Which may explain why boats' rigs are so complicated. Over the centuries, sailors have found a myriad of ways to improve their vessel's sailing performance – sometimes to make their work easier, sometimes to reduce wear and tear, but more often to make it go faster. This chapter looks at the major elements of the rig as well as some of those fine-tuning devices.

SAILS

It's fair to say that no area of sailing technology has developed as dramatically in recent years as sail construction. The revolution started in the 1950s, when synthetic materials such as Dacron replaced cotton as the material of choice. Dacron had the advantage of being cheap, strong and able to hold its shape. What's more, it put up with all kinds of abuse, including being put away while still wet – something that could spell the end of a cotton sail. After Dacron came laminated sailcloth which combines layers of synthetic fibre with super-strong material such as Kevlar to produce a variety of cloths to suit different sailing situations.

It's not just the cloth that helps a sail keep its shape, but the way it's stitched (or even glued) together. Long before Dacron was invented, sailmakers tried to minimise stretch by using narrow panels of cloth stitched together parallel from the bottom of the sail upwards. From the mid-1950s onwards, triangular foresails were stitched with panels at 90° to each other to take advantage of the natural strength of woven cloth. With the advent of laminated sailcloth, sailmakers can orientate panels in a way that reflects the loads in the sail, and they can even vary the thickness of each panel according to how much load it will be subjected to. The result is a light, incredibly strong and, above all, low-stretch sail that is every racing sailor's dream.

TOP LEFT: The first generation of modern sails, made of Kevlar and similar, look stunning – although the sails on this Malaysian yacht have been stitched together in simple horizontal panels.

BOTTOM LEFT: A good set of modern cruising sails, probably made of Dacron and stitched from narrow panels to minimise stretch. Full-length battens in the mainsail help it keep its shape.

TOP RIGHT: The 1896 cutter Avel carries a spectacular 2,000sq ft (185m²) of sail. The mainsail has narrow horizontal panels to imitate traditional canvas sails, but the foresails are all 'mitre cut' (ie panels stitched at 90° to each other) to give better performance.

BOTTOM RIGHT: The new generation of sails, such as on the modern classic yacht Chloe, are laminated rather than stitched. This allows the sailmaker to change the direction of the material and its thickness depending on the loads in the sail.

SPINNAKERS & POLES

Not all sails need to be flat. While sailing upwind is all about creating the most efficient aerodynamic foil, sailing downwind is all about scooping up as much wind as possible with as big a sail as possible. Enter the spinnaker. This is by far the biggest sail on a boat – the largest spinnaker on the Volvo Round the World Ocean Race yachts is twice the size of a tennis court. This giant sail is traditionally set in front of the boat and is used to sail directly downwind. A spinnaker pole is used to adjust the angle of the sail to the wind, and a complex system of lines is needed to control both the pole and the sail.

Sailing directly downwind, however, isn't necessarily the fastest way to get from A to B. Despite the extra mileage, it's usually faster to sail at a slight angle to the wind in a series of broad reaches. Which is why the asymmetric spinnaker was created. Rather than floating in front of the boat, the asymmetric is attached by one corner to its bow (usually on a short retractable bowsprit) and billows out on the leeward side like a giant, bulbous genoa. It's relatively easy to control and less likely to cause the boat to broach dangerously. And it's fast. For all those reasons it's rapidly taken over from the traditional spinnaker as the downwind sail of choice.

TOP LEFT: Asymmetric spinnakers have been around for some time, but have recently come back into fashion. Note how the corner of the sail is attached to the boat's bowsprit, rather than floating in the air.

TOP RIGHT: A traditional spinnaker, where the same corner (the 'tack') is attached to a spinnaker pole and the whole sail hovers well in front of the boat. This is a better sail for sailing dead downwind.

BOTTOM: A fleet of Sunsail yachts storm down the Solent, off the Isle of Wight, during a recent Round the Island Race. These are 'tri-radial' spinnakers designed for sailing straight downwind.

SPINNAKER SHAPES

A star-cut spinnaker is narrower on top and better for reaching; a radial head is full at the shoulders and better for going downwind; a tri-radial is mid-way between the two. Most older spinnakers were cross-cut.

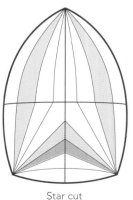

Star cut
spinnaker

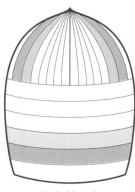

Radial head
spinnaker

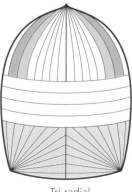

Tri-radial
spinnaker

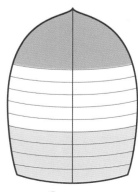

Cross cut
spinnaker

REEFING

No one's invented a sailboat with a brake yet, so when the wind gets up and the boat starts heeling over too much, the only thing to do is to reduce the area of sail. There are three ways of doing this. A conventional mainsail is fitted with several lines of reefing points, running parallel with the bottom of the sail. The sail is partially lowered, the reefing points are lashed around the foot of the sail (using reef knots, of course) and the sail is reset. It's a fiddly business which usually involves being thrown about by the boom rather a lot.

A slightly easier method is roller reefing, whereby the entire boom is rotated and the sail rolled around it until it's the right size – although, as the rolling mechanism is located next to the mast, you're still likely to get your feet wet. Easier still is slab reefing, which is entirely controlled from the cockpit and is great for short-handed sailing, though it does leave an ugly pile of sail stacked up on the boom.

Until the early 1900s, there was no easy way of furling foresails, so if the wind got up the crew had to go on deck and hoist smaller sails. Then in 1907 Major Wykeham-Martin patented his roller-furling system, which consisted of a bronze spool which spun the front edge of the sail, rolling it around itself. Not only was it quick and easy to use, but it could be controlled from the cockpit – which meant no more dangerous trips to the foredeck. The system, now used on 99% of yachts, has been improved and refined since but is essentially the same as Wykeham-Martin devised more than 100 years ago.

ABOVE: A traditionally reefed yacht. The bottom of Hardy's sail is furled and secured using a line of reefing points. Two more lines are available should the sail need to be reduced further.

TOP LEFT: A roller-furling mechanism fitted to the end of Dirk II's bowsprit by means of a traveller (see p76).

TOP CENTRE: In-mast furling is an easy way to reduce the size of a boat's mainsail. The sail simply rolls into the mast.

TOP RIGHT: Wykeham-Martin invented the original roller-furling mechanism which this, and all others, are based on. As the sail is unfurled, the line rolls into the barrel. To stow the sail, simply pull the line, which rolls the barrel in the opposite direction.

BOTTOM: There's no time to fiddle around with reefing points when you're racing around the world. Ellen MacArthur's yacht Kingfisher was fitted with slab (or 'jiffy') reefing, whereby the bottom two corners of the sail are pulled taut, and the rest is left to fend for itself.

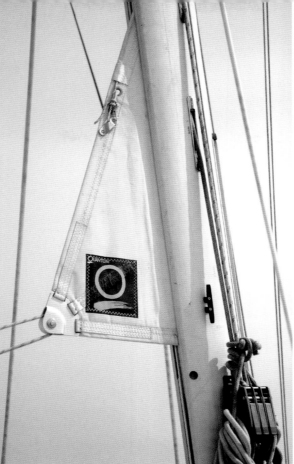
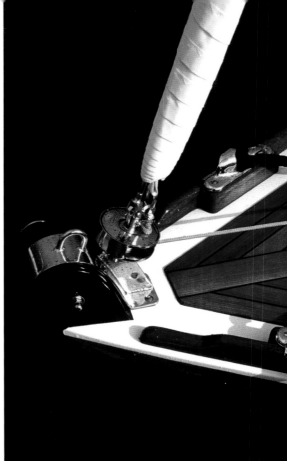

MASTS

It's reassuring to know that standards to regulate most aspects of boatbuilding have been laid down by respectable agencies such as Lloyd's and the American Bureau of Shipping (ABS), even if those rules are only voluntary. The one area that neither body has dared rule on, however, is the construction of masts and rigging – which says a lot about the black art of mast design.

The principles are simple enough. Stick a wooden pole on a boat and you have a mast you can raise your sail on. Add rigging to support the pole, and you can reduce the thickness of wood by more than 80%. Add spreaders (horizontal struts which increase the angle between the rigging and the mast) and you can reduce the mast thickness still further. And that's before you've even looked at stronger modern materials such as aluminium (since the 1960s) and carbon fibre (since the 1990s). In fact, by the time you've got onto carbon fibre, you've gone full circle and can afford to get rid of all that other stuff and just fit a simple carbon fibre pole – which is exactly what designer Nigel Irens did when he drew his anachronistic (and soon iconic) lugger *Roxanne* in 1994.

The organisers of the 2013 America's Cup have gone a stage further. They have fitted their catamarans with wing sails – effectively aerodynamic wing-shaped extensions of the mast. As the fixed sails need less force to control them, the boats themselves can be lighter, which means… Well, you can see where this is going: you end up with a 131ft mast on a 72ft boat. Now what would Lloyd's and the ABS have to say about that?

ABOVE: Aluminium masts are relatively cheap and low-maintenance – and surprisingly strong, as this picture of a Sigma 38 being dragged over by her spinnaker shows.

OPPOSITE, TOP LEFT: Launched in 1996, Stealth was the first yacht built entirely of the new wonder material carbon fibre – including her 125ft (38m) mast.

TOP RIGHT: This is something you don't see very often: a catamaran with a mast on each hull – described as a 'lateral schooner'. Does it work? The jury's still out, but first impressions are 'no, not really'.

BOTTOM LEFT: Before the invention of carbon fibre, a tall mast could be made even taller by adding a topmast. In heavy weather, the topmast could be lowered (or 'reefed') to reduce weight aloft.

BOTTOM RIGHT: The latest America's Cup boats have wing masts which act like the wings of an aeroplane. This is the AC45, the junior version used for the trial series; the wing on the AC72 used for the Cup proper is as big as the wing of a Boeing 747.

SPREADERS

Some boats have one, two, three, four, or even five, and some have none at all. The logic behind spreaders – horizontal struts which stick out on either side of the mast – is not easy to pin down.

The purpose of spreaders (or crosstrees) is to increase the angle between the rigging (or shrouds) and the mast, to give greater sideways support to the mast. This means that not only can the mast be made of lighter stuff, but the rigging can be thinner too, reducing the overall weight of the rig. Spreaders also allow the shape of the mast to be adjusted. For, while it might seem like the purpose of all that rigging is to keep the mast straight, the masts on most modern racing yachts are 'pre-bent' by as much as 12in (30cm), so that they bulge forward in the middle. This not only prevents the mast flexing but also flattens the sail, which is particularly helpful when sailing upwind. Once under way, the amount of bend in the mast can be adjusted depending on conditions, using the backstay tensioner.

BELOW: It wouldn't be possible to make a mast this tall and this thin without spreaders. Spreaders break the mast down into sections (called 'panels') which can be stacked on top of each other like building blocks.

As for how many spreaders a boat should have, that depends on what it's being used for. Most cruising yachts with aluminium masts will have two, while modern racing yachts with tall floppy masts might need as many as four or five. At the other extreme, some Open 60 racing yachts fitted at deck level with rotating masts had a single pair of enormous spreaders. But then, as I said, spreaders aren't easy to pin down.

TOP: Some Open 60 racing boats were fitted with rotating masts which were extremely aerodynamic. Instead of traditional spreaders, they fitted these enormous deck spreaders to ensure there was a big enough angle between the mast and the side rigging ('shrouds').

HOW SPREADERS WORK

Each 'panel' is supported by a 'diagonal', which runs from the base of one spreader to the end of the spreader below it. The cap shroud runs from the top of the mast down to the side of the boat.

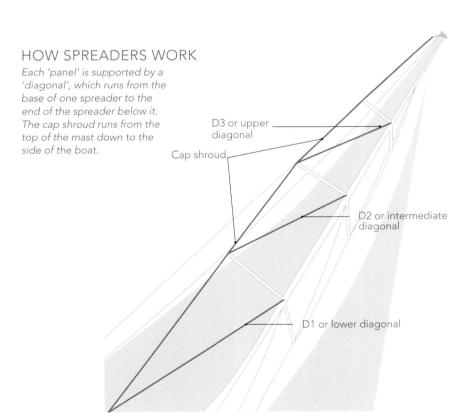

D3 or upper diagonal

Cap shroud

D2 or intermediate diagonal

D1 or lower diagonal

STANDING RIGGING

Just as masts have followed a virtuous circle of becoming increasingly light and increasingly strong, so standing rigging (the stuff that supports the mast and helps keep it in shape) has followed a parallel path. A hundred years ago, when wood was the standard material for masts, galvanised steel wire was the norm for standing rigging. From the 1960s, as masts switched almost overnight to aluminium, standing rigging switched equally abruptly to stainless steel wire – or, if you were really swish, solid stainless steel rod, from the 1970s. And that, it seemed, was the natural order of things.

Then, in the 1990s, the new generation of high-tensile fibres came on-stream and turned everything upside down. Suddenly, the old correlation between strength, weight and rigidity was thrown out of the window and you could have a material that was incredibly strong, light and flexible. Fibre standing rigging is 50% stronger and yet 70–80% lighter than its stainless steel counterpart. Similarly, a carbon fibre mast is 40% lighter than an aluminium one. All this weight saving means you can reduce the amount of ballast needed to balance the boat, which means you need less sail area to drive the boat, which means you need less standing rigging – and you're into another virtuous circle.

That said, stainless steel rigging and aluminium masts will be around a while longer – not because of any emotional attachment to them, but because of another less virtuous beast: cost.

ABOVE: Tough steel wire has been replaced by fibre on high-performance yachts, such as this Open 60. The cables are made of materials such as Kevlar, carbon fibre and PBO, while the fittings are often made of titanium. Modern fibres are much stronger and much, much lighter than their steel counterparts.

RIGHT: The 135ft (41m) schooner Eleonora makes an impressive sight from the air. Most yachts nowadays are rigged using stainless steel rigging, but owner Ed Kastelein decided to use traditional galvanised steel. Why? Because it's more reliable and less likely to break without warning.

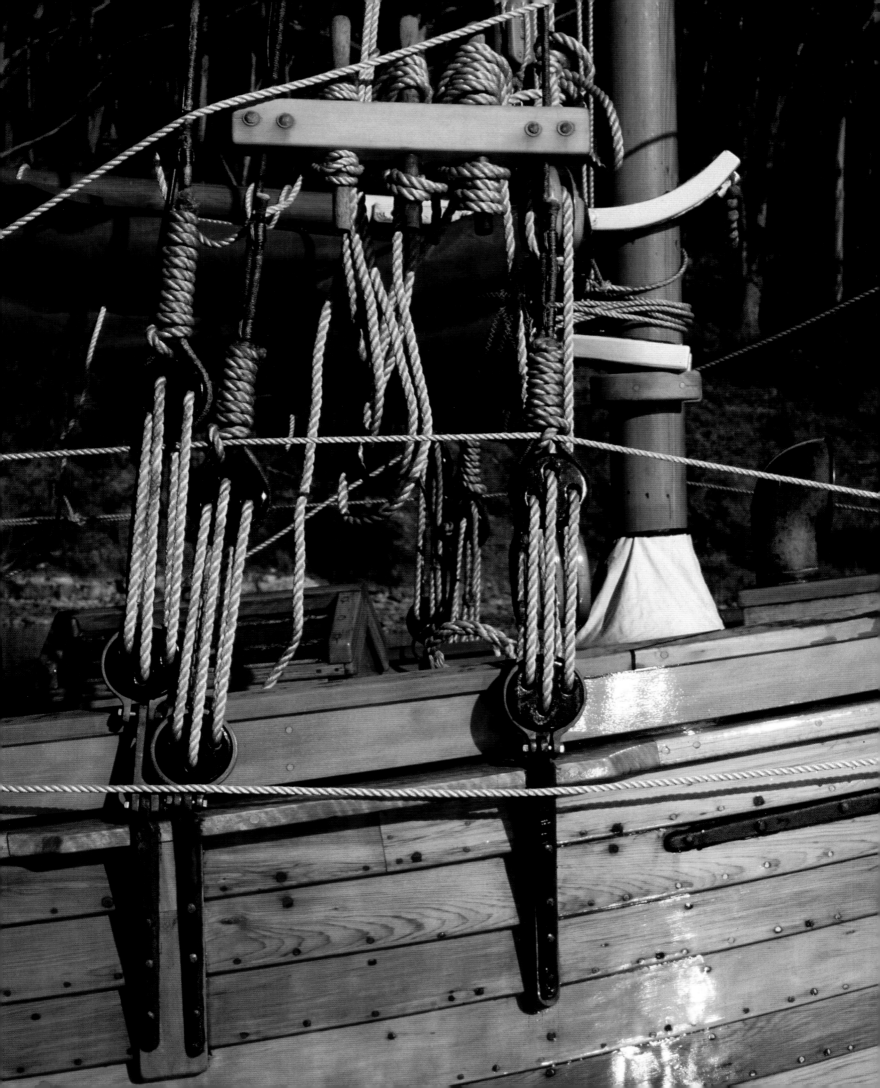

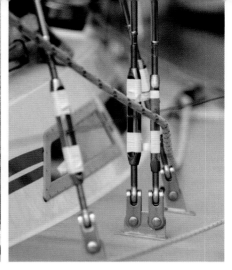

TERMINALS

OPPOSITE: This might look like something from another era, but it's the terminals of a wooden boat built on a beach in Tasmania. Rather than buy expensive bottlescrews, builder Mike Seeney made Madoc's deadeyes (the round black circles) and lanyards himself.

TOP LEFT: Bronze bottlescrews are the preferred option on most classic yachts, for their reliability and ease of use. Acrospire's wire rigging has been spliced, wrapped in twine and tarred in the traditional manner.

TOP CENTRE: A neat backstay tensioner on a modern cruising yacht. The tension on the rig – and therefore the shape of the mast – can be instantly adjusted by pumping the lever.

TOP RIGHT: The norm. The vast majority of modern yachts are rigged with stainless steel rigging tightened with stainless steel bottlescrews attached to stainless steel chainplates.

It might be a term more commonly associated with pianos, guitars and car engines, but a yacht's rigging also needs to be tuned. In fact, so important is this process on bermudan yachts that some races could be said to have been won or lost before the boats even left the dock – through skilful or unskilful tuning. Nowadays, this is mostly done by adjusting the bottlescrews which link the lower ends of the rigging wire to the hull. The screws are adjusted in strict order – usually making sure there is no lateral bend in the mast, before introducing some pre-bend fore-and-aft to improve the shape of the sail. With the advent of fibre stays, however, bottlescrews are becoming a thing of the past. Instead of adjusting the standing rigging manually, the ends are attached directly to the hull and the tension is adjusted by raising or lowering the mast with a hydraulic jack.

It's all a long way from the methods used on traditional ships such as the *Cutty Sark*. Here, the ends of shrouds were attached to deadeyes – thick circles of wood, usually made of lignum vitae – which were attached to the ship with lanyards. To tension the shroud, the lanyard was pulled tighter and lashed down. It's a method still used on some classic yachts, as much for practical as aesthetic reasons. By the time stainless steel rigging came along in the 1960s, though, most yachts had long since converted to bottlescrews. Which was just as well, as by then the combined effects of modern rigs and fibreglass hulls meant that rig loads had increased dramatically, and the rigging needed to be similarly inflexible.

RATLINES & MAST STEPS

No self-respecting book or movie about pirates would be complete without a few ratlines thrown in for good measure. There's something irresistibly salty about the word (pronounced 'rattlins'), and they even look suitably piratical in real life. Indeed, Sturdy Ratlines is one of the mission rewards on the computer game *Pirates of the Burning Sea*, because, as it points out, 'With well-maintained ratlines, the crew can quickly move about the rig to adjust sails and yards.'

Which is exactly what ratlines were originally designed to do. Long before roller-reefing and in-mast furling gear, the crews of the great square-riggers had to climb up the ships' masts to furl and unfurl the sails, and ratlines were what enabled them to do this. Most ratlines were made of manilla and had a habit of breaking after a certain time, which is why crew were told to trust their hands and not their feet when climbing aloft. Nowadays, they are mainly fitted on traditional boats for maintenance purposes and on long-distance cruising yachts, where a high vantage point might be needed to spot underwater obstacles while navigating unfamiliar waters. They can be made either of rope and lashed to the rigging, or of wood and bolted or lashed.

ABOVE: A good set of sturdy wooden ratlines on the 1902 schooner Coral. *The steps have been notched at either end and then lashed in place with twine.*

OPPOSITE, TOP: On square-riggers, sails have to be furled and unfurled by sailors climbing up the rigging. A series of ratlines are rigged between each set of sails, with footropes strung out under each yard for sailors to walk out on.

OPPOSITE, BOTTOM: Designer Daniel Bombigher specialises in piratical-looking little ships, so it's no surprise Drum of Drake *is fitted with ratlines on both masts. As well as making maintenance easier, they allow the crew to keep a lookout for rocks, whales – and treasure.*

HANKS & SLIDES

Since the invention of an efficient roller-reefing system for genoas in the 1970s, followed a couple of decades later by in-mast furling, you might think that sail hanks are a thing of the past. Think again. None other than the Volvo Ocean Race fleet fitted hank-on foresails for their state-of-the-art round-the-world racing yachts in 2008–9, and many other top racing yachts do likewise. The reason? Reliability and performance. Hanked-on sails are less likely to jam or become detached and, when reducing sail, swapping the headsail for a smaller one will usually give a better sail shape than using roller-reefing. The disadvantage is the time it takes to change sail – but then you're not usually counting the seconds when you're racing around the world.

Likewise the mainsail. While in-mast furling is popular with cruising folk and novice sailors, it has yet to convince everyone. For one thing it means the bottom of the sail can't be attached to the boom; for another most systems can't be used with sail battens – both of which are extremely detrimental to the shape of the sail. Which is why most mainsails are still attached to the mast and boom using traditional methods such as: a bolt rope stitched to the edge of the sail which slides in a groove in the mast or boom; slugs which slide in a groove; or slides which slide in (or on) a track attached to the mast or boom. It may be a while before sailors are ready to completely abandon their hanks, slugs and slides.

TOP: The mainsail on the biggest gaff cutter in the world, Lulworth, is 5,000sq ft (465m^2) – that's nearly twice the size of a tennis court. The bottom of the sail is secured by dozens of small slides which slide on a metal track attached to the boom.

BOTTOM LEFT: Before roller reefing there were hanks. The front edge of this jib is hanked onto the forestay to keep it taut.

BOTTOM CENTRE: The sides of the mainsail on this modern cruising yacht are attached in two ways. The bottom (or 'foot') has a boltrope stitched to the edge of the sail which runs through a groove in the boom, while the side (or 'luff') is attached to slugs which slide up a groove in the mast.

BOTTOM RIGHT: Another method is simply to lace the sail to the boom with a long line, such as on the 1889 classic yacht Thalia.

BANDS & IRONS

It says a lot about modern materials that spar bands are more or less a thing of the past. Whereas every fitting attached to a wooden mast or boom needed some sort of band or iron to spread the load, most of the fittings for aluminium spars can be bolted straight into place or, in the case of carbon fibre, moulded into them during construction. In some cases, fittings have been eradicated altogether. Why bother with crude attachments for sheet blocks when you can simply fit a couple of 'soft' loops, made of Spectra or Dyneema or somesuch, around the boom and attach the blocks to those instead?

For owners of wooden boats, however, mast bands and irons are very much a day-to-day reality – and indeed several companies specialise in manufacturing nothing else but exquisitely beautiful (and wincingly expensive) bronze fittings for every part of a sail boat's rig. And it can get pretty esoteric. There are peak halyard bands, topping lift bands, clew bands, sheet bands, cranse irons, gammon irons, and bowsprit heels, not to mention goosenecks, gaff saddles and travellers (covered elsewhere).

With the advent of aluminium spars in the 1960s, most of these were remoulded in either aluminium or stainless steel and simply riveted to the spar. It wasn't pretty and it was impossible for the amateur to repair without specialist tools, but from the manufacturing point of view it was cheap to assemble and extremely durable. Almost overnight, it was goodbye mast bands, hello pop rivet gun.

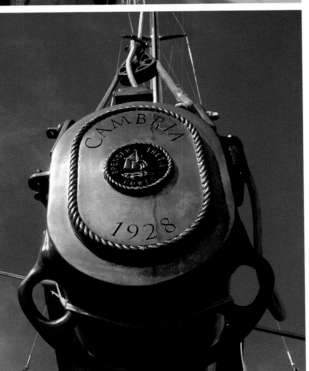

OPPOSITE PAGE, TOP: This sheet block is attached to the wooden boom with a metal band which is tightened around the boom with a single bolt. The block itself is hooked onto the bolt, with a lashing (or 'mousing') to stop it jumping out.

BOTTOM LEFT: A more sophisticated system is this stainless steel hoop (or 'bail') which is either screwed or through-bolted onto the boom. The shackle slides along the hoop, allowing the sheet block to self-adjust.

BOTTOM CENTRE: Traditional gaff and boom bands on the West Country ketch Irene.

BOTTOM RIGHT: Aluminium masts ushered in a new era of mast and boom fittings manufactured out of stainless steel or aluminium and riveted in place.

THIS PAGE, TOP: Thanks to the wonders of Spectra and Dyneema, soft loops now replace metal bands on many yachts – software instead of hardware.

BOTTOM: Even a boom band can become an object of beauty, such as this bronze boom end fitting on the classic yacht Cambria.

BOWSPRITS

1

Why do some boats have bowsprits and others not? Historically, it was mainly a matter of displacement (ie weight) and sail shape. Traditional wooden sailboats were heavy beasts and needed a lot of sail to get them moving. Increasing the sail area upwards increased weight aloft and moved the sails' centre of effort up, neither of which was desirable. Increasing sail area sideways with the addition of a bowsprit not only kept the weight of the rig and its centre of effort low, but also allowed the mast to be moved forward thereby reducing the vessel's weather helm (ie tendency to turn into the wind).

It was the introduction of the bermudan rig, combined with improved (read 'lighter') boatbuilding techniques, which spelled the end of bowsprits on modern boats for half a century. The centre of effort of a triangular sail is by definition further forward, which means the mast had to be moved back and the foresails brought inboard, eliminating the need for a bowsprit. Almost simultaneously, the arrival of lighter aluminium masts meant weight aloft was no longer an issue. Some bermudan-rigged boats carried on having bowsprits, but for other reasons: perhaps for anchor stowage or to reduce the height of the mast for trailer towing purposes.

The return of the asymmetric spinnaker has breathed new life into the bowsprit. Suddenly, even the coolest racing yachts are sprouting shiny black 'sprits. They are usually made of carbon fibre and therefore need no stays, and slide away imperceptibly into the boat's hull in order not to attract additional marina fees.

5

1. It's good manners to retract your bowsprit when moored in a public place, like this Irish hooker in Galway, to avoid tangling your neighbour's mooring lines.
2. This aluminium bowsprit has probably been 'reefed' to reduce the boat's berthing fees.
3. The bowsprit on this bawley replica is a single solid piece of Douglas fir.
4. Safety first: a net has been stretched under this bowsprit and wire 'jacklines' fitted for the crew to clip onto.
5. Climbing to the end of the bowsprit usually provides the money shot – as long as you don't mind getting dunked.

6. This one is 24ft (7m) long…
7. A neat stainless steel bowsprit that simply folds away.
8. Bowsprits have become popular again in recent years thanks to the return of the asymmetric spinnaker, pioneered by J Boats such as this.
9. They can be used for other things, such as attaching a figurehead.
10. Even round-the-world racing yachts such as this Open 60 now have bowsprits.
11. This carbon fibre bowsprit retracts into the boat itself.

DOLPHIN STRIKERS

Whiskers and dolphin strikers are to the bowsprit what spreaders are to the mast. That is, they increase the angle of the stay, giving them more leverage and strengthening the whole arrangement. The dolphin striker (or martingale) works with the bobstay under the bowsprit, while the whiskers work with the shrouds on either side of the bowsprit. Whereas on masts the minimum angle between the rigging and the mast is 10°, this is often impossible to achieve on bowsprits unless whiskers and dolphin strikers are used. The alternative is to beef up the bowsprits and stays, adding more weight at the bow of the boat where it is least wanted. So ultimately, whiskers and dolphin strikers save weight.

Although dolphin strikers had their heyday in the 19th century, when some square riggers even experimented with double martingales, they made a comeback 150 years later with the resurgence of sports catamarans such as Hobie Cats and Tornados. The mast of these boats rests on the forward crossbeam, exerting a great deal of downward pressure, especially when going over a wave. Rather than add extra weight by building a stronger crossbeam, a dolphin striker is placed under the beam directly under the mast, with stays attached to each end of the beam. This converts the force into a compression load, rather than a buckling load, which means a lighter crossbeam can be fitted. So once again, the dolphin striker saves weight.

TOP LEFT: The mainsail is reefed, the jib and flying jib are stowed – the pressure on Moonbeam's rig is enormous as the yacht powers down a wave off Cannes. The whiskers and dolphin striker (partially submerged) keep the bowsprit steady and ultimately support the top of the mast.

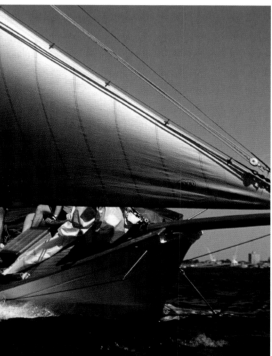

TOP RIGHT: Dolphin strikers, like bowsprits, have had a sudden resurgence thanks to the popularity of sport catamarans – and America's Cup yachts, such as this AC42. This boat is fitted with two dolphin strikers: one under the mast, the other under the forestay strut. A long bobstay joins the two, running from the end of the bowsprit to the rear crossbeam.

BOTTOM LEFT: The 1897 classic yacht Sayonara, racing in Port Phillip Bay off Melbourne. The yacht was given a million-dollar restoration in 2000, including fitting new bronze whiskers and dolphin striker. With a sail area of 1,763sq ft (164m²), her rig needs all the support it can get.

BOTTOM RIGHT: Another classic yacht from 'down under', this time the 1907 Waione, which beat all comers when she was returned to gaff rig in 1999. She has no whiskers and only a short dolphin striker, which only slightly changes the angle of the bobstay. This isn't unusual in a boat of her size (just 30ft 8in (9.35m) on the waterline), where the loads are much less.

  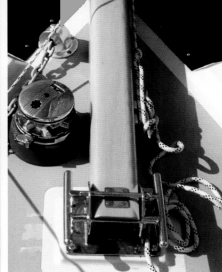

BITTS

The loads on a bowsprit are, as might be expected, enormous. Imagine the force generated upwards and sideways by the jib in a strong wind, then add the force of waves crashing over the bow and you get an idea of what's involved. Not surprisingly, bowsprits can and do get broken regularly. The best way to prevent this is to minimise sideways movement of the spar through the use of stays: a bobstay from the tip of the bowsprit to the stem, and shrouds on either side. The aim is to transmit as much of the load as possible to the heel – just as the load of a mast is transmitted to its foot. The heel is in turn held between the bitts: two massive posts which run through the deck to the keelson below. A metal pin, or fid, usually holds the heel in place and can be knocked out when the spar needs to be 'reefed'.

So much for traditional gaffers. On modern boats, the bitts are usually replaced by a metal fitting bolted straight to the deck. In order to keep marina fees to a minimum, bowsprits have to be retractable, and a considerable amount of ingenuity has been spent devising heel fittings which can facilitate this process. One small gaffer has a bowsprit which goes through a porthole in the forward end of the cabin, and out through the saloon, while others are hinged at the heel to allow them to be hoisted upwards into the rigging.

TOP LEFT: A classic set-up on a British East Coast smack: the bowsprit runs between the bitts, with a roller on top and a leather underneath to ease its progress. The hole where the pin (or 'fid') is passed through to lock the bowsprit is just visible.

TOP CENTRE: A metalworker's interpretation made of galvanised steel. The heel of the bowsprit fits between the bitts, with the locking fid clearly visible this time. A complicated arrangement of cleats clutters the top of the bowsprit.

TOP RIGHT: The modern gaffers don't need bitts: a simple stainless steel bracket bolted to the fibreglass deck will suffice. The only drawback is that, once the pin is removed, the bowsprit has to be lifted out of the bracket before it can be slid inboard.

OPPOSITE: Because of their intrinsic strength, bitts are often used for other purposes, such as the base of an anchor windlass. The block and tackle visible on top of the bowsprit is used to haul the spar out after it's been stowed inboard.

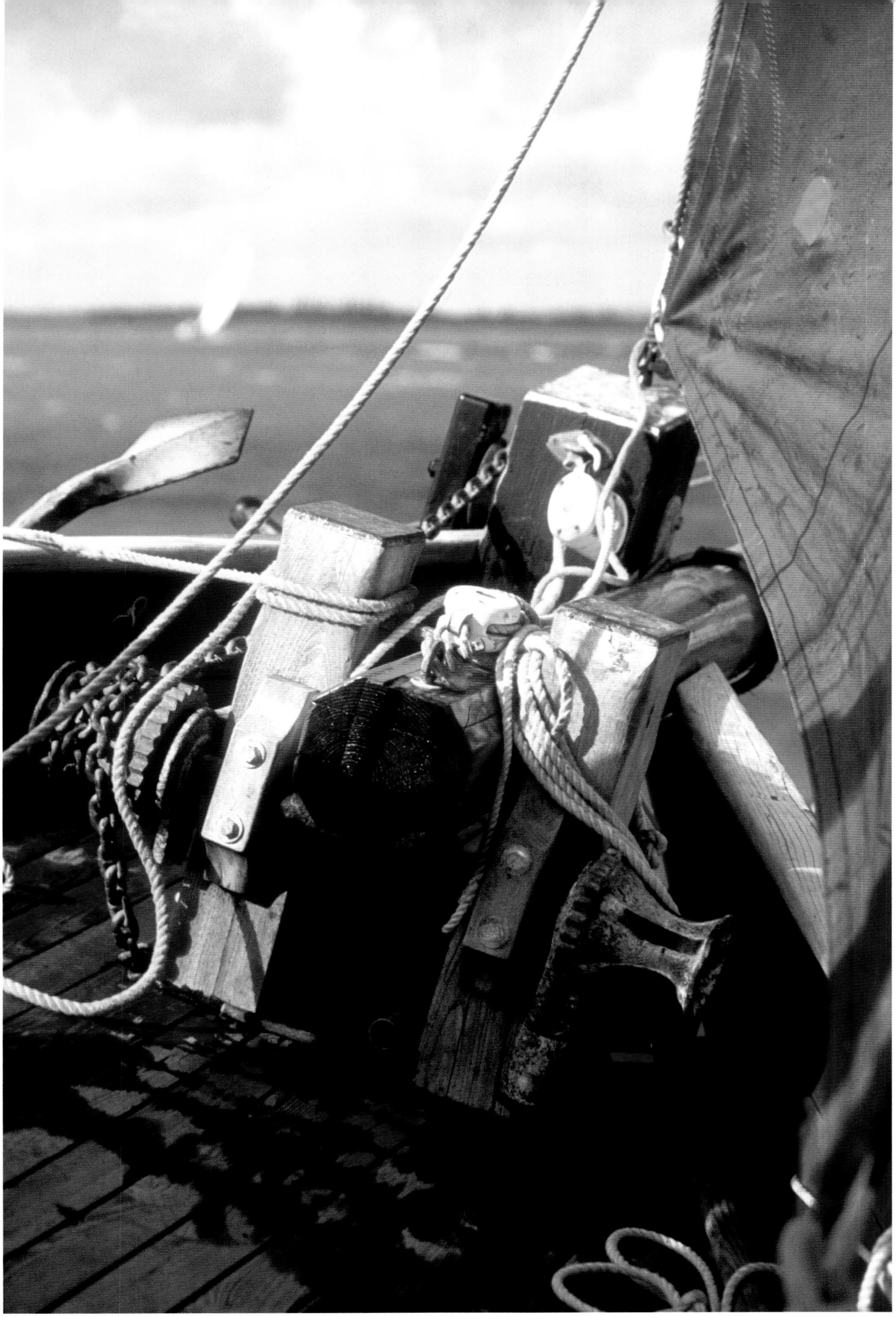

BOWSPRIT TRAVELLERS

Bowsprits are wonderful things, but attaching a sail to the end of one is like taking part in a greasy pole competition: you're pretty much guaranteed to get a dunking. One solution is a bowsprit traveller, which does exactly what its name suggests: travels up and down the bowsprit.

A traveller is typically a steel ring, usually covered with either rope or leather to reduce chafe, fitted with two loops: one to attach the sail to, the other for the 'outhaul' line. The outhaul line runs through a roller (or 'sheave') set into the outboard end of the bowsprit and back to a cleat located on or near the inboard end. Once the jib is attached, the traveller is pulled to the end of the bowsprit using the outhaul, and the line is cleated off. With the base of the jib in position, the halyard can then be hauled tight and the sail set in the usual manner.

When the jib needs to be retrieved, the halyard is released and, once the sail has been brought under control, the outhaul is released and the sail itself used to slide the traveller back to the boat. The sail is then detached and stowed in a sail bag. All without even getting a toe wet!

TRAVELLER ARRANGEMENT

The traveller is one of many components fighting for space at the end of the bowsprit of the 1885 classic yacht Partridge. *It requires careful planning to make sure everything runs smoothly.*

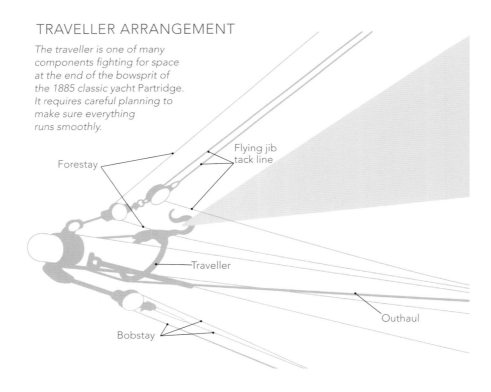

Forestay

Flying jib tack line

Traveller

Outhaul

Bobstay

The 1885 cutter Partridge charges down the Solent, sailing again for the first time in 60 years after her landmark restoration.

BUMKINS

A bumkin is really just a bowsprit fitted to the other end of the boat. Whereas the bowsprit is attached to the forestay and allows an extra sail to be set at the front of the boat, the bumkin shifts the aft stay further aft and allows a longer boom. This is particularly useful on traditional boats with low-aspect rigs and heavy spars, where the weight of the rig needs to be kept as low as possible. In this case, it makes sense to fit a longer boom and increase sail area sideways rather than upwards. Modern boats with lighter rigs can afford to raise the height of the mast, and bumkins have all but disappeared from mainstream use.

One area where bumkins (also known as bumpkins or boomkins) do still find favour is among long-distance cruising folk. A V-shaped bumkin made from two pieces of wood not only frees the aft deck by moving some of the rigging out of the way but also provides a useful attachment point for a variety of gadgets, such as self-steering gear, windvane, lifebuoys, etc. It can even be used as a short gangplank for climbing on and off the boat while moored stern-to the dock.

78

OPPOSITE: This 1930s yacht has a bermudan rig and wooden spars. The short bowsprit forward and the bumkin aft means the sail area is kept low, which in turn reduces weight aloft.

BELOW: Pushing this idea to the extreme, the sail area on this smuggling ship replica is kept low by spreading it out between two masts and an extremely long bowsprit and bumkin. This configuration suits her hull shape.

BOOMS

One of the most terrifying words anyone can hear aboard ship is the cry of 'Boom!' That usually means a long, heavy pole is careering towards your head at speed, intent on making grievous contact with your skull. It might sound like a silly cliché, but many sailors have been injured in this way, sometimes fatally, and sailors are trained to have a Pavlovian reaction to the call of 'Boom!'. Try shouting it in the bar next time you're out drinking with a bunch of sailors, and watch as at least half the assembled crew duck their heads nervously.

Booms, like masts, come in all shapes and sizes. Wood (preferably spruce) was the default material on yachts until aluminium came along, with steel finding favour on the big square riggers. Now, for those who can afford it, carbon fibre is the material of choice, being 45–65% lighter than aluminium and several times stronger. And, whereas boom shape used to be limited by the materials available (usually round or rectangular), all kinds of fancy, streamlined shapes can be created out of carbon fibre at the touch of a button, using the latest computer-guided technology. One result is the return of the so-called Park Avenue boom. Pioneered in the 1930s by the J-Class yachts as a means of controlling the shape of the mainsail, they can now be built with a deep V-section into which the sail can be neatly flaked as it is lowered, simplifying the whole stowing process.

OPPOSITE PAGE, TOP: This aluminium boom has a groove on top for the foot of the sail and a groove underneath for the sheet and vang fittings.

CENTRE: A light carbon fibre boom such as this needs a vang (see p84) to prevent the boom lifting on downwind legs.

BOTTOM: A Class 40 racing yacht fitted with carbon fibre spars.

THIS PAGE, BELOW: Carbon fibre booms can be made in all shapes and sizes.

BOTTOM: The weight of a heavy wooden boom helps the sail keep its shape on downwind legs.

GOOSENECKS

The gooseneck's job is relatively simple: to hold the boom in position against the mast. Of course, life is never quite that easy, and the fact that the boom needs to swing horizontally by as much as 90° on either side of the mast while being subjected to huge vertical loads by the sail (pulling up) and the sheet (pulling down) means it needs to be a fairly hefty bit of kit.

As the name suggests, the original fitting was simply a vertical bar which the boom was hooked onto, not unlike a brass or steel goose's neck. This was fine as long as the boat was sailed off the wind, but as sails became more sophisticated and boats were sailed closer to the wind (ie more upwind), the loads on the gooseneck increased, and something more robust was required. On wooden spars, this comprised a couple of mastbands and a pivot, while on aluminium boats the gooseneck was either riveted directly to the mast or, on smaller boats, set on a slide on the sail track. The advantage of the latter was that the luff of the sail could be tensioned using a downhaul, which meant a halyard winch wasn't required. And so gooseneck development stood still for half a century or more, until the arrival of carbon fibre. Now, the gooseneck can be built into the mast itself, and all that's needed is to fit the boom and lock it in place with a pin. Simple, neat, and massively strong.

TOP LEFT: As well as holding the boom in place, this gooseneck holds the rollers (or 'sheaves') for the reefing lines ('pennants') that run through the boom. The hooks on either side hold down the corner of the sail (the 'tack') when it's reefed.

TOP CENTRE: The traditional gooseneck rotates on a pin held at either end by a pair of mast bands. This one has a couple of belaying pins neatly built into it.

TOP RIGHT: A traditional bronze gooseneck fitted on a dinghy. The boom slides up and down the bar, allowing the front edge of the sail ('luff') to be tightened with a downhaul.

OPPOSITE PAGE: This gooseneck fits into the hollow aluminium boom, where it is riveted in place, and then joined to the mast. It also provides the attachment point for the corner of the sail (the 'tack').

VANGS

ABOVE: A hydraulic vang fitted to the 78ft (24m) Maxi sailing yacht Farniente. Sailing close to the wind, the outside edge of the sail ('leech') is kept in tension by the sheet. Off the wind, as the boom is eased out, the sheet has less effect and the vang takes over.

There's a V-jam, a cascade, a fiddle, a cascaded fiddle, a cascaded kicker and even, for the seriously competitive, a double-ended cascaded kicker. These are all types of vangs fitted to sailing boats of all sizes – from run-of-the-mill dinghies to state-of-the-art racers.

The vang has two main functions: to tension the outer edge of the sail leech and to keep the boom under control in adverse conditions. At its simplest, it can be just a block and tackle running from the underside of the boom to the base of the mast. Increasingly common are solid vangs, which are used in conjunction with a block and tackle and can support the boom when the sail is lowered, meaning no topping lift is required. On larger yachts, the block and tackle is usually replaced by a hydraulic or electric pump.

Tightening the vang has the effect of tensioning the luff of the sail and bending the mast back slightly, which helps windward performance. Off the wind, the vang stops the boom lifting up and spilling the wind out of the sail, as well as preventing it see-sawing when the boat rolls. On the other hand, if the boat is hard-pressed in a gust, it pays to release the vang to spill the wind and depower the sail.

Vangs of this type are rarely fitted to gaff-rigged vessels, partly because the weight of the boom is thought to do the job adequately, and partly because gaffers are not designed to sail close to the wind anyway.

ABOVE: The old-fashioned way. The black line on the right does the same job as the vang opposite, only you'll have to pull the tail end to make it work. The red line on the left is the mainsail sheet, which in this case is led forward to the mast, then back to the cockpit.

CRUTCHES & GALLOWS

Even with the sails lowered, a yacht's boom is still a potentially lethal weapon, especially in rough weather, and needs to be tethered securely as quickly as possible. On the vast majority of vessels built after the 1950s, this is done by hardening up the topping lift and hauling in the mainsheet as tightly as possible. Trouble is, unless you've fitted the latest high modulus cordage, both lines are likely to stretch and, as the boat rocks gently on her mooring, the boom will swivel in its gooseneck, gradually wearing away at the pin. The situation is even worse if you've got a wooden boat with a long heavy boom and stretchy lines.

Which is why many traditional sailboats were (and are) fitted with either crutches (which fold away) or gallows (which are fixed). Both bits of kit allow you to secure the boom firmly, once the sail is lowered and the topping lift released, making sail stowage easier and safer and eliminating wear and tear on the gooseneck when not under way. The main drawback of gallows is that they are likely to get in the way, although they are often fitted with handholds which add another safety factor. Both methods also have the added benefit of ensuring the topping lift won't part one day and dump that boom right on your head.

OPPOSITE: Nothing fancy about the boom crutch on this $1.6m classic yacht – but it does the job. The jaws are leathered to protect the boom, and the feet have softwood pads to protect the deck. The yacht's name? Vanity V.

TOP RIGHT: These gallows on the Italian yawl Agneta are quite ostentatious by comparison, with three positions for the boom and a lot of fancy metalwork. In a strange reversal of priorities, the notches are lined with metal.

CENTRE RIGHT: An elegant solution on the American 1938 sloop Mercury, in the form of a simple bronze hoop mounted with a wooden block to protect the boom. Most of the yacht's fittings appear to be original.

BOTTOM RIGHT: A less fancy version of the Italian gallows, with three notches on the crossbeam (not lined with metal) and bronze uprights (not polished). The posts have handholds in the top corners, adding a safety element.

The 1912 gaff cutter The Lady Anne sails back in her home waters on the Firth of Clyde in Scotland. Her rig is extended by a slender topmast which fits directly onto the top of the main mast.

YARDS & GAFFS

If you like your sails to be triangular in shape, then masts and booms are all you need. In which case, read no further. If, on the other hand, you like the idea of strange rhomboid- and trapezoid-shaped sails, then you'll need a whole bunch of other spars too. Welcome to the world of gaff, lug, sprit, and square sails – and many others besides.

The first sailboats were no doubt square-riggers, setting a simple square sail from a horizontal yard attached to the mast. That eventually developed into the mighty square-riggers of the 18th and 19th centuries, which carried dozens of sails set on dozens of yards set on up to five masts. At some point, sailors worked out that, by setting the sails in line with the hull (ie fore-and-aft) rather than perpendicular to it, and changing the angle of the yards, they could sail higher into the wind than with a square sail. Thus the lug rig was born. From there, it was a small step to actually pivoting both yards on the mast to create the gaff rig.

But the first fore-and-aft rig in the world was the lateen rig, which developed in the Mediterranean at about the same time as the claw rig was evolving in the Pacific. A version of the lateen rig made its way to Holland where, legend has it, a clever boatbuilder stepped the top yard into his vessel's thwart and did away with the mast altogether – creating the precursor to today's bermudan rig. Which is how we got triangular sails.

TOP RIGHT: The yard of a lug rig crosses the mast and is hoisted up on a traveller (a metal loop which circles the mast). The sail sets best on the leeward side of the mast and therefore has to be lowered and reset every time the boat changes tack.

UPPER CENTRE: The top spar (called the 'gaff') on a gaff rig butts against the mast, which means the sail sets correctly whichever side the wind is on. A 'crane' holds the blocks and halyard clear of the mast.

LOWER CENTRE: The horizontal spars on a square-rigged ship are called the yards. Crews have to climb along them to furl and unfurl the sails – or they can just sit down and enjoy the view.

BOTTOM: Thames barges are powered by enormous spritsails. A single spar (called a 'sprit') runs from the bottom of the mast to the outermost corner of the sail (the 'peak'). Rather than lowering the sail, it is furled against the mast ('brailed') with brailing lines.

JAWS & SADDLES

Jaws or saddle? That is the question for anyone contemplating a new or replacement spar on a gaff cutter. Like a boom, the gaff needs to pivot on either side of the mast, following the angle of the sail. Unlike a boom, the gaff also has to be hoisted up the mast and then 'peaked' (ie made more vertical) while the sail is being set, usually starting at 90° and finishing at 30–45°. It's a tall order to achieve this amount of mobility using traditional materials, but two solutions have emerged: jaws and saddles.

Jaws are usually made of solid oak or laminated from a hardwood such as Canadian rock elm or iroko, and can readily be made by the DIY boat owner. The inner face is lined with leather to prevent chafe and, on bigger boats, sometimes fitted with a 'tumbler', a hinged pad which stays flat against the mast at all angles. The ends of the jaws are loosely tied around the mast with a parrel line fitted with parrel beads, ideally made of lignum vitae.

Saddles are usually made of steel or bronze and are generally too complicated for home manufacture. Unlike jaws, they are unlikely to ever break and, on high-peaked gaffs (ie those with a smaller angle between gaff and mast), are less likely to twist and 'fall off'. They are generally heavier than jaws, however, and a good deal more costly.

You pays your money and you takes your choices… Either way, don't forget to slap on a dollop of Vaseline to ease the gaff's passage up the mast. It will also stop that annoying squeak.

TOP: Gaff jaws keep the top spar on a gaff sail attached to the mast, while allowing it to rotate freely. Larger gaffs such as this one are sometimes fitted with a 'tumbler', a hinged piece of wood on the inside face of the jaw, which spreads the load over a greater area than the jaw alone.

OPPOSITE: A traditional gaff rig set-up on the 1945 Greek caique Faneromeni. The leather on the mast protects it from chafe, while the parrel beads allow the jaws to slide up and down the mast with ease. A dollop of Vaseline or similar is advised to keep the whole thing running smoothly.

ABOVE: Gaff saddles do the same job as jaws but are manufactured from steel or bronze. The saddle is hinged to keep it flat against the mast as the gaff is hoisted and 'peaked'. The long, twisted eye or 'stirrup' on this saddle ensures the shackle doesn't scrape the mast when the spar is raised.

HOOPS & LACING

Another dilemma for gaff sailors is: hoops or lace? (And no, this has nothing to do with earrings or petticoats!) The question is how best to attach the luff (ie the forward edge) of the sail to the mast, bearing in mind you can't fit a sail track on a gaff rig. Mast hoops made out of 2½ turns of ash, riveted together and then leathered, are the traditional solution. Others advocate steel hoops, which are heavier than wood and tend to droop but also much less likely to break. Either way, there is something very traditional about a pile of hoops neatly stacked at the foot of a mast (when lowered) or stretched up a mast (when raised). Trouble is, they break quite easily and are virtually impossible to replace once the mast is raised – which is why sensible riggers always add a couple of spares when the mast is lowered.

The other solution to the luff question is rope lacing. A long length of line is either lead round the mast and through the cringles in a spiral or, preferably, backwards and forwards through the cringles and around the forward face of the mast. Advantages: lighter, pulls the sail closer to the mast, can be fitted with the mast up, costs a fraction of the price of mast hoops. Disadvantages: may snag (though much less with the 'backwards and forwards' method above), can't be used as a ladder to climb the mast. There would be no contest really, were it not for the undeniable romance of mast hoops. And sailors are a romantic lot.

TOP LEFT: Mast hoops or lace? There's no denying mast hoops look good, but they also have drawbacks, not least being almost impossible to replace once the mast is up. On the plus side, they are handy for climbing the mast should the need arise.

BOTTOM LEFT: Lacing isn't as traditional-looking, but has the advantage that it can easily be adjusted or replaced at any time. The riggers of this Irish hooker have used the 'backwards and forwards' lacing technique, which is less likely to snag than the 'round and round' method.

OPPOSITE: Each mast hoop is a minor work of art. Two-and-a-half rounds of ash are steamed around a circular former and riveted together. They are then varnished before the forward part is covered in leather and laboriously cross-stitched. The leather is then treated with lanolin or similar.

BLOCKS

It's no exaggeration to say that blocks make the sailing world go round. And never more so than during the Age of Sail, when hundreds of blocks of all sizes were needed to control the maze of spars and sails of the great square riggers. So important were they, that the world's first production line was set up in 1805 to produce standardised blocks for the Royal Navy.

Blocks have two main purposes on a yacht: to change the direction of a line and/or to give mechanical advantage. At their simplest, a line of single blocks might be used to lead a roller furling line back to the cockpit along the side of the boat, so that it doesn't snag anything on deck. More impressively, high-tech blocks are used on modern racing yachts to control sails in extreme conditions, often being subjected to loads of several tons. A simple four-part block and tackle will allow a sailor to quadruple their effort, and modern materials, such as carbon fibre and nylon sheaves, make the system increasingly efficient.

Although pulleys have been in use since at least 1500 BC, when the Mesopotamians used them to haul water out of wells, it was Archimedes who first realised their full potential in around 230 BC, when he used them in ships to allow sailors to control large loads, such as stowing cargo, handling the sails or hoisting particularly heavy items like the anchor. It has even been suggested that the blocks used by Nelson's ships contributed to his victory at Trafalgar, as the English fleet outmanoeuvred the French, using blocks to raise and lower their sails and help with countless tasks on board.

1. Modern blocks often use ball bearings to help the sheave run more smoothly and increase the efficiency of the system.
2. There are no winches on the 1911 classic yacht Tonino, so blocks are used wherever possible.
3. Even the line on this traditional Russian replica is made of hemp.
4. Ash is the timber of choice for blocks' cheeks. Customised caps can be added to off-the-shelf blocks, or they can be made in-house by the boatyard.

5. Three single blocks are used here in preference to triple blocks, presumably to spread the load.
6. Five blocks are needed to hoist just one end of one gaff on this 80ft (24m) schooner Coral; then there's the topping lift, the topsail sheets…
7. Some functional blocks at the base of a modern cruising yacht.

1

4

TURNING BLOCKS

The combined effect of incredibly strong modern lines and powerful winches may have reduced the need for complicated pulley arrangements to control a yacht's sails, but modern yachts are still bristling with blocks and multi-coloured lines. So what are they all for? One reason for all this extra cordage is safety – or, some would argue, comfort. Whereas in the past sailors were quite happy to dance around on the coachroof heaving at halyards and tying off endless lanyards while being clobbered by a heavy boom, nowadays most people would prefer to reef their sails from the comfort of the cockpit. This means three sets of reefing lines (pennants, or pendants) have to be run along the boom, down the mast, along the coachroof and back to the cockpit. Likewise many other lines that used to be operated from the foot of the mast, such as halyards, topping lifts, downhauls, etc.

A key component of this trend of bringing running rigging back to the cockpit are turning blocks – essentially a block with a fixed point of attachment, rather than the usual becket and shackle arrangement. They've been around for a long time in various forms, though the long lines of multiple blocks filled with a dazzling array of colour-coded lines is a more recent development. Safety or comfort? The answer is: both!

OPPOSITE PAGE, TOP LEFT: All the running rigging on this modern gaffer is led back to the cockpit, resulting in a cluster of blocks at the base of the mast and lines of turning blocks on the coachroof.

TOP RIGHT: This turning block neatly incorporates a jammer, which means the line can be adjusted on the winch without fear of it pulling away.

BOTTOM: A typical sight on most modern sailing yachts: a series of turning blocks feed the running rigging back to the cockpit. This allows the sails to be raised, lowered and reefed without leaving the cockpit.

THIS PAGE, BOTTOM (LEFT): Cylindrical ball bearings minimise friction on this turning block. (CENTRE): A turning block fitted to a track allows the sheeting angle of a sail to be adjusted. (RIGHT) The traditional equivalent: a bronze turning block finished in leather on a bronze track.

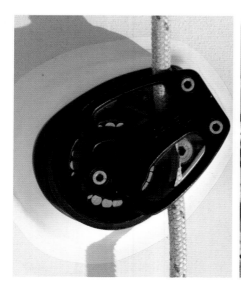

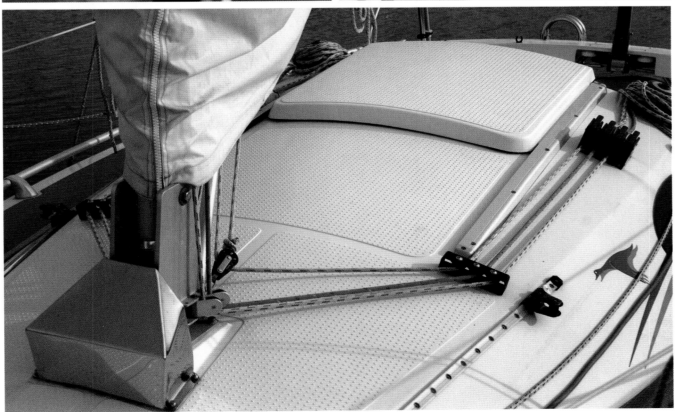

MAINSHEET TRAVELLERS

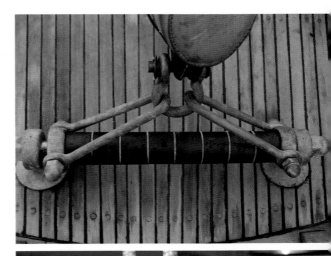

Traditionally, the purpose of the traveller is to move the pulling point of the mainsheet so that it's more directly under the boom. This prevents the boom lifting and flattens the sail somewhat, something that's particularly important on gaff-rigged yachts not fitted with vangs. It works like this. The lower mainsheet block is attached to a 'car' which slides along a bar (or 'house') or track attached to the deck. Each time the boat changes tack, the car slides over the leeward side (ie the side the sails are on), placing it closer to the boom. Because gaff sails aren't very efficient if sheeted in too close to the centre of the boat, there's no need to control the car; it simply sets itself.

The arrival of the bermudan rig changed all that. Not only does a bermudan mainsail operate very well close to the centerline, but sail shape has a dramatic effect on performance, particularly to windward. The sheeting point is crucial to all this. The car on a modern traveller therefore has blocks on either side to allow it to be adjusted depending on what shape is needed. In light winds, the traveller can be set on the windward side, allowing the boom to be sheeted in without flattening the sail too much. In strong winds, the traveller can be centred and the mainsheet sheeted in to flatten the sail. Off the wind, the traveller is set on the leeward side, and the vang does most of its work.

OPPOSITE, TOP LEFT: On a modern racing yacht, such as this Pogo 12.5, the traveller (controlled by the blue line) is used to control the angle of the sail, while the sheet (the orange line) is used to control the shape of the sail.

BOTTOM LEFT: A stainless steel 'horse' on a 1960s bermudan sloop. Here, the block is allowed to slide to the leeward side, and the sheet is used to control the angle of the sail.

TOP RIGHT: The purpose of this mainsheet buffer is to absorb some of the enormous loads transmitted by the gaff mainsail.

CENTRE RIGHT: The modern equivalent is this traveller, with a carriage fitted on a track which runs almost the full width of the yacht.

BOTTOM RIGHT: A 1930s carriage and track arrangement on Solway Maid.

WINCHES

Winches are so ubiquitous on yachts, it's easy to assume they've been around for ever. And indeed they have been used in the form of large, ungeared capstans for weighing anchors and raising sails since at least Nelson's day. Once the sails were raised, however, they had to be adjusted by hand using only blocks and tackle.

The first recorded use of winches for controlling a vessel's sails while under way was in the 1903 America's Cup. The American defender for the Cup that year was *Reliance*, which still holds the record as the largest gaff cutter ever built. That means that instead of having two or more masts with lots of small sails, she had a single mast with a few very large sails. In order to control these huge sails, *Reliance* was fitted with winches below decks. These winches used a system of cogs to give a mechanical advantage which enabled her crews to operate loads far greater than would have been possible using blocks alone.

By the 1930s, winches had evolved into the compact units we are used to seeing today, although it wasn't until after the Second World War that they became affordable to the general public. Since then, the materials have evolved – from bronze to aluminium to stainless steel to carbon fibre – but the essential design has remained unchanged. Perhaps the biggest development is the self-tailing device fitted to the top of the winch, which frees both hands to turn the handle.

1. *Lewmar have been making winches since 1950. This stainless steel Astor is their top-of-the-range racing model.*
2. *An aluminium Lewmar winch dating from the 1970s.*
3. *Merriman bronze winches were among the first mass-produced winches and were ubiquitous on yachts from the 1930s onwards.*
4. *Adjusting the line in the self-tailing mechanism.*
5. *Self-tailing winches allow the crew to use both hands to turn the handle.*

6. *A vintage winch fitted on the 1931 Sparkman & Stephens schooner Brilliant.*
7. *A bronze Lewmar self-tailing winch.*
8. *Several different types of handle attachment were tried out, including these raised studs (ouch for the toes!), before the current design was settled on.*
9. *A modern self-tailing winch from Harken, with modern synthetic line.*
10. *The Danish company Andersen have been making winches for 60 years.*

PIN RAILS & BELAYING PINS

If a big square-rigger carries in the region of 50 sails and each sail has on average three lines to control it, then that means there must be about 150 cleating points on deck to attach those lines to. That's a lot of belaying and coiling! In fact, a close study of the cleating plan (yes, there is such a thing) of the 1905 four-masted barque *Pamir* (apparently the last commercial sailing ship to round Cape Horn) suggests that's an underestimate; the *Pamir* has 150 cleats per side, or 300 in total. Rather than making countless cleats, however, the builders of such ships fitted pin rails: hefty lengths of timber attached to the vessel's bulwark and pierced with dozens of belaying pins, to which the lines were attached. Alternatively, the pin rails could be attached to the standing rigging – usually to the lower part of the shrouds – while other, free-standing rails were fitted around the base of the mast, in which case they were known as Fife rails.

Pin rails are very practical as they clear the running rigging away from the mast, which is why they are still fitted to many traditional yachts and even some modern cruising yachts. Debate still rages about the best place to fit them, with some arguing that attaching them to the rigging places the load in the wrong place and can damage the shrouds. Few will disagree, however, that they are very salty bits of kit or, as every pirate knows, that those belaying pins make a mighty fine weapon.

TOP RIGHT: Pin rails at the base of the mast are known as Fife rails. Legend has it the name comes from a type of flute – the Fife rail being the place the fifer would play a tune while the anchor was being raised.

CENTRE RIGHT: Pin rails are usually fitted to the ship's bulwarks, which clears the running rigging away from the mast.

BOTTOM RIGHT: This free-standing bronze pin rail is fitted to the 1923 classic yacht Astor. The belaying pins are fixed, and eyes have been built into the bolts.

OPPOSITE: Another option is to bolt them to the base of the shrouds, which gives maximum clearance but arguably puts an unnecessary extra load on the rigging.

JAMMERS & CLUTCHES

One result of the current trend of bringing as many rigging lines as possible back to the cockpit might have been a lot of cleats cluttering up the crew's seating area, were it not for the ingenious line jammer. This neat device holds the line with a simple lever, usually pulled down towards the crew. One of its main advantages is that it doesn't require the crew to tie any knots – which means you're less likely to have the mainsail unceremoniously dumped on your head in the first puff of wind. A slightly more sophisticated version of the jammer is the line clutch, which does essentially the same thing but allows the line to be tensioned once it is loaded. It's more bulky and expensive than a jammer, but is now ubiquitous on every modern yacht.

Crucially, however, both jammer and clutch should only be used for relatively static lines, such as halyards and topping lifts, which don't usually need to be released in a hurry. The long-standing favourite for sail sheets is the cam cleat, which can be easily incorporated into a sheet block and can be yanked free in a split second. This is not to be confused with the clam cleat, which is more prone to jamming and is generally only used with smaller more static lines, such as flag halyards, centreboard lines and suchlike. Or even a jam cleat, which is a cleat with an angled horn which the line can be jammed into. Confused? When it comes to jammers, as elsewhere, a picture is worth a thousand words…

1. *A cam cleat works by squeezing the line between a pair of spring-loaded cams. These cams are made of Tufnol, an early type of laminated plastic invented in the 1920s.*
2. *Sheet leads and jammers vie for space on this Clipper round-the-world racing yacht.*
3. *A line of clutches on a modern racing yacht. With so many lines, it's a good idea to label all the clutches.*
4. *An unusual bronze jammer on the 1902 schooner Coral.*
5. *A neat arrangement of bronze cam cleat and wooden mainsheet block on a stainless steel mount.*
6. *The line is simply wedged tight on this traditional bronze clam cleat.*
7. *Clutches are usually fitted forward of the winch, so one winch can operate several lines.*
8. *A pair of modern cam cleats, with reinforced plastic cams.*
9. *At least a dozen lines come back to this one winch, operated by a single person on this Open 60 racing yacht.*

RUNNING RIGGING

The fibre revolution of the past 20 years has transformed the shape, look and feel of sailing: carbon fibre is replacing aluminium in masts, Spectra replacing nylon in sails, and composite sandwiches of exotic materials replacing fibreglass in hulls. One of the most shocking changes, however, is in running rigging (the stuff you use to hoist sails and control them once they're up). Whereas 50 years ago the problem was finding rope that was strong enough for the job without being too bulky, the new generation of ropes are so strong they are too skinny to handle, and some sailors are choosing overstrength ropes just to have something to hang on to.

This has had a dramatic knock-on effect on the amount of rope needed to operate a boat. Back in the days when manila was the standard issue, all running rigging had to be run through a complex network of blocks to spread the load and gain mechanical advantage. Even now, square riggers such as the 234ft (71m) barque *Eagle* need about six miles of running rigging to operate all their sails. Up until recently, the mainsheet on most yachts was still made up of a six-part block and tackle with six turns of polyester rope. Thanks to the strength of ropes such as Dyneema and PBO, combined with the power of modern winches, that can now be reduced to a single loop running through a single block on the boom. Less than a generation ago, that would have been unimaginable.

OPPOSITE, TOP: Sweating the running rigging the traditional way, on the 1915 Baltic trader Circe. Old boats have lots of strings for paying guests to pull.

BOTTOM: This would have been unimaginable 30 years ago. Instead of the usual multiple blocks with multiple wraps of the mainsheet, this Pogo 12.5 has a single line (in red) passing through a single block at the end of the boom. That line is used by the crew with the light blue jacket to control the shape of the sail. The angle of the boom (ie the power) is controlled by the traveller at the back of the cockpit (the line in blue, being untangled by the crew with the red hat).

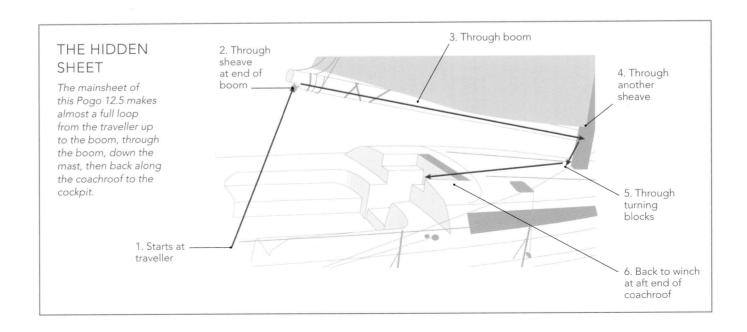

THE HIDDEN SHEET

The mainsheet of this Pogo 12.5 makes almost a full loop from the traveller up to the boom, through the boom, down the mast, then back along the coachroof to the cockpit.

1. Starts at traveller
2. Through sheave at end of boom
3. Through boom
4. Through another sheave
5. Through turning blocks
6. Back to winch at aft end of coachroof

4 ON DECK

What can beat that first moment when you step on board an unknown vessel? Straight away you get a sense of the boat's power by the movement (or lack of it) generated by your own weight – a mathematical equation calculated in the soles of your feet. Next, a quick look around to appreciate her deck structures, such as cabin trunks, hatches and cockpits, which are so integral to the character of a craft. And then you can indulge in a long lingering examination of all the other intriguing details which make the boat work efficiently or otherwise. It might not be as good as a first kiss, but it comes pretty close.

CABIN TRUNKS

Just as hull design is often a dainty dance balancing the conflicting demands of speed, safety, comfort and aesthetics, so designing deck structures is usually a series of compromises. First there is the coachroof height, which must provide adequate headroom within without looking too boxy from without; then there's the size of the cabin trunk, which must leave enough deck space so the crew can get about the boat safely while providing enough space below decks.

When it comes to the details of styling, however, it's all down to aesthetics – for, as far as we know, no one has yet been killed by an ugly cabin. There are a few ground rules every designer should observe, as spelled out by America's Cup guru Ted Brewster. The coachroof should have a flatter curve than the sheer and point towards the tip of the bow. It should be roughly parallel to the waterline or rise slightly towards the stern – never the other way. The sides of the cabin should angle in slightly (a minimum of ¼in (6mm) per foot (30cm) is recommended), otherwise, even if they are vertical, they will look as if they are angled outwards. And the line of portholes should follow a line midway between the sheer and the top of the coachroof.

Of course, many modern designs throw all these rules out of the porthole and have flush or extremely raked cabins and yet still manage to look graceful. But then you have to know the rules before you can break them.

TOP LEFT: In the 1970s, wedge-shaped cabins, such as on this half-tonner, became popular, throwing out conventional wisdom about what made a pretty design.

BOTTOM LEFT: The rounded cabin trunk and gently curved coachroof of this 1923 Australian classic yacht epitomise the best design principles of the era.

OPPOSITE, TOP: The modern compromise is a wide, well-angled coachroof, stretching far forwards, such as on this X-45 'performance cruiser' built in Denmark.

OPPOSITE, BOTTOM: A more radical approach is this flush deck on the 78ft (24m) Maxi yacht Farniente. It might not appeal to everyone, but it's certainly uncluttered.

COCKPITS

It's often said the kitchen is the heart of a house, and similarly the cockpit is the heart of a boat. The challenge for designers is that cockpits serve two very different purposes. Under way, they are the vessel's control centre, from which the sails are adjusted, the helm is steered and commands emitted. Once the anchor is dropped, they turn into outdoor living rooms, where crews sit around socialising, eating, sunbathing and, in warmer climes, sleeping.

Size is the starting point. A boat needs a large cockpit for all that late-night socialising, but it must also be narrow enough so that the crew seated on the windward side can brace their feet on the leeward side when the boat is heeled over. It should be big enough to convert into two comfortable berths, but small enough that if the boat is pooped it won't be sunk by the weight of water inside the cockpit. The sole must be low enough that the seats are ergonomically comfortable, but high enough so that it is above the waterline when the boat is heeled to allow the drain to work. The seats should be high enough so the crew can see over the cabin, yet low enough so that they are not too exposed to the elements. The seat backs should be angled so the crew on the windward side are not tipped out of their seats when the boat heels over, yet not so angled that they are uncomfortable when eating their dinner once the sailing's over.

And that's just the start. Designing a cockpit makes juggling look easy!

RIGHT: An uncompromising double racing cockpit on the 1933 classic 12-Metre Vema III. The helmsman has his/her own position, while the crew work the sheets from the main cockpit. Lounging is not an option.

BOTTOM LEFT: Four people are crowded into the cockpit of this 33ft (10m) cruiser/racer, with two more on the leeward rail. The helmsman has to stand up and hold the tiller extension to get a clear view ahead.

BOTTOM CENTRE: The deep coamings (sides) and beautiful craftsmanship on the cockpit of the classic yacht Integrity are deeply appealing. However, the narrow footwell means it will get crowded if there are more than two or three people.

BOTTOM RIGHT: Open stern cockpits, such as on this French JPK1010 design, save weight and allow water to drain out quickly. They're also susceptible to 'pooping', and are not usually used on long-distance cruising yachts.

HATCHES

Everyone loves a butterfly skylight – as long as it's on someone else's boat. There's something quintessentially classic about this double-leafed hatch, with its handsome wooden frame and protective brass bars running across the glass. And some great minds have applied themselves to fine-tuning the concept, including designers such as Olin Stephens, Francis Herreshoff and Bruce King. Yet despite this, they still have a reputation for leaking – usually along the hinge line – which is why they are best admired from a distance. That said, the modern alternative of aluminium or stainless steel frames with tinted perspex glass may be more efficient, but they are brutally ugly by comparison.

A belt and braces approach is required for the foredeck, which sooner or later is likely to be pounded by heavy waves, if not completely immersed in the sea. Here, the winning formula was devised by yacht designer Maurice Griffiths, who came up with the idea of the double coaming hatch. He accepted that water might come through the first joint and fitted an inner coaming with a channela between the two as a kind of baffle for the water to run down. Simple but effective – like most of Griffiths's ideas. Once again, the modern alternative looks brutal by comparison: a heavy-duty frame bedded on neoprene with some sturdy plastic levers to seal the deal. Still, if it keeps your bunk dry, it's probably preferable to any amount of varnished teak or mahogany.

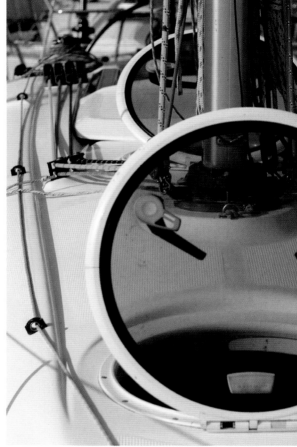

DOUBLE COAMING HATCH

Maurice Griffiths's hatch design has an inner coaming to keep the water out, with a gap between the coamings and a scupper for the water to run through.

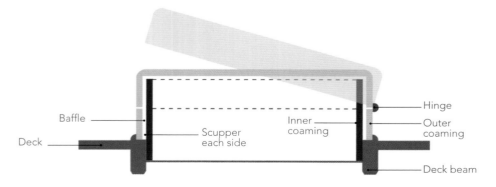

Baffle

Deck

Scupper
each side

Inner
coaming

Hinge

Outer
coaming

Deck beam

TOP LEFT: A double coaming hatch with sturdy bronze hinges, intended to keep out Atlantic storms. This 1960s sloop raced 2,500 miles from the UK to the Azores and back.

LOWER LEFT: These modern hatches let in a lot more light, but don't offer any protection from spray when they are open.

TOP RIGHT: A belt-and-braces approach has been taken with these 'fortified' butterfly skylights. The gutters down which the water is supposed to run are visible under the hinges and on the bottom edge of the frame.

BOTTOM RIGHT: This flush, tinted hatch on a luxury modern yacht is less obtrusive and probably more watertight than a traditional skylight, but also lets less light in. Non-skid strips should be stuck on the glass to prevent the crew slipping over while stowing the mainsail.

WHEELS

When Leif Ericson sailed to Newfoundland in AD 999, he used a tiller. And when, 500 years later, Columbus sailed the ocean blue too, he used a whipstaff. For these were the only ways of steering a vessel, until the ship's wheel was invented in about 1703. Once it had been conceived, the wheel revolutionised sailing, allowing craft of any size to be easily controlled. Along with the anchor, it soon became the defining icon of ships and sailing.

The design of the ship's wheel has changed remarkably little since then. Although the wheel on a modern America's Cup yacht might be made of carbon fibre, the design is still fundamentally the same as wheels fitted by the Royal Navy 300 years ago. Granted, it's more likely to be used to trigger a hydraulic mechanism than to haul on ropes and pulleys, but the essence is unchanged. It remains to be seen whether today's lightweight miracles become as popular on the walls of pubs and bars as their historic forebears.

1. *Lightweight carbon fibre is the material of choice for these double wheels (one each side) on a modern racing yacht.*
2. *This large bronze and wooden wheel on the 1938 racing yacht Seven Seas looks pretty stylish, but is a much later addition.*
3. *A traditional wooden wheel fitted on the modern steel barge yacht Juno.*
4. *The historic ship's wheel of the 1845 Portuguese frigate Dom Fernando II e Gloria. The line on the drum is linked via wooden blocks directly to the tiller.*
5. *The smart stainless steel wheel on the J-Class yacht Velsheda is twice the size of her original wooden wheel.*

6. *Modern materials allow designers to modify traditional designs, such as the bendy spokes on the 1998 modern classic Wild Horses.*
7. *Bronze wheels are cold in winter, so are best fitted with wooden handles.*
8. *It certainly looks 100% traditional, but this wooden wheel is fitted on a replica classic yacht built in 2004.*
9. *Stainless steel is also cold in winter, which is why stainless steel wheels are usually given a protective cover in colder climes.*

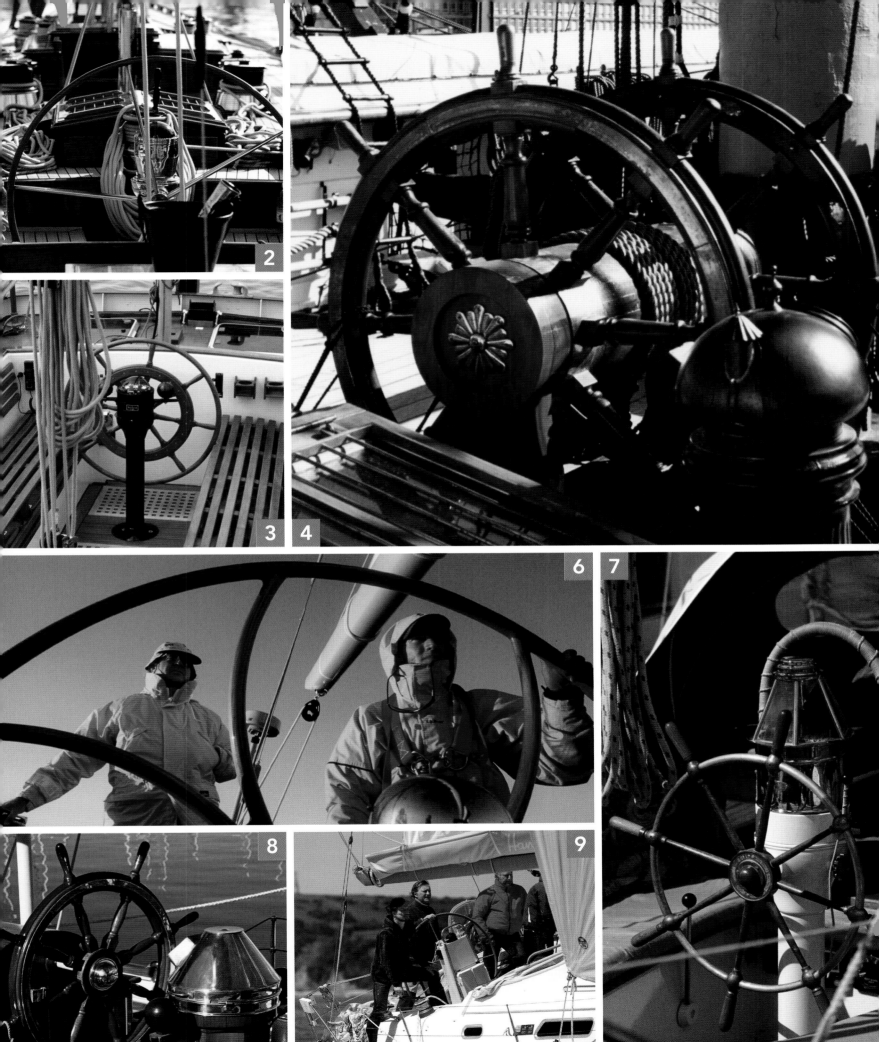

TILLERS

It might seem a strange anachronism that any yachts are still fitted with tillers. After all, the ship's wheel has been around for at least 300 years and offers far greater mechanical advantage and therefore ease of steering. Not only that, but it's more compact and therefore friendlier to the cockpit crew than a great sweeping tiller. Yet many of the most cutting edge racing yachts, including the trial boats for the last America's Cup series, are fitted with tillers. Not only that, but they are usually made of wood – indeed, they are usually the only bits of wood amid an ocean of carbon fibre and epoxy.

The reason usually given for preferring a tiller over a wheel is the feel of the thing. The tiller connects the helmsman to the vibrations in a yacht's hull in a way that a wheel steering system never can. It's been compared to driving a manual rather than an automatic car, and the advocates of each approach are usually as vociferous as their road-bound counterparts.

Not that anyone agrees on what shape a tiller should be, or even what length. On traditional boats, it usually curves over the aft deck in a gentle arc into the cockpit. On modern boats, it usually rises from the cockpit sole in an elegant 'S' shape, to clear the cockpit side when it turns. Either way, mechanical advantage is measured by the distance of the handle from the rudder stock, so the longer the tiller, the greater the mechanical advantage. Too long, however, and it's likely to disembowel the cockpit crew.

BELOW RIGHT, TOP: Probably the only piece of wood on this modern racing yacht. This tiller is laminated from ten strips of wood to create a precise S shape.

BELOW RIGHT, BOTTOM: Getting the tiller past the mizzen mast can be a problem on boats with stern-hung rudders. The builder of this 15ft (4.6m) Sea Otter has come up with an innovative solution. Note the carving at the end of the tiller – an otter of course!

TOP LEFT: Olympic sailor Ben Ainslie helms a 45ft (14m) America's Cup catamaran using a tiller. The 72ft (22m) version used for the Cup itself was fitted with wheels.

BELOW LEFT: At the other end of the scale, the 28-ton classic yacht Partridge is steered using a long wooden tiller. The end is carved with a monkey's fist knot.

5 FITTINGS & EQUIPMENT

Nathanael Herreshoff was a clever man. Over a period of 40 years he designed more winners in the top races of the day, including five America's Cup winners in a row, than all his rival designers combined. But as well as designing some of the most spectacular boats ever built, he also lavished care and attention on the minutiae of yacht hardware. He is credited with inventing the sail track and the modern sail winch, and the Herreshoff cleat is still produced to this day. That's because he knew that even the most expensive boat could be disastrously let down by a seemingly minor piece of equipment. When you're at sea, every link in the chain counts.

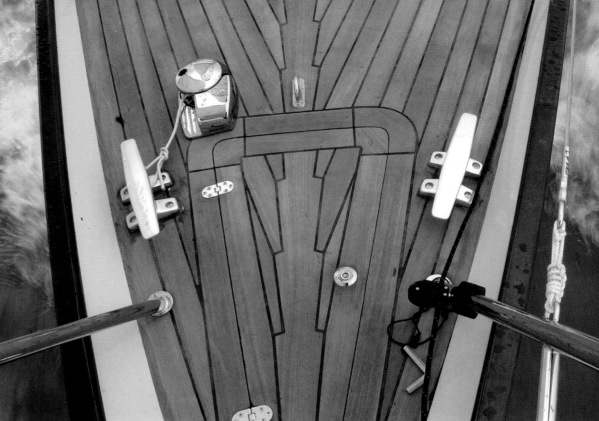

CLEATS

TOP LEFT: Making a wooden cleat is easy when you know how – but potentially disastrous if you get it wrong.

ABOVE CENTRE: The ubiquitous aluminium cleats fitted to most modern cruising yachts: strong, light and cheap.

OPPOSITE PAGE, ANTICLOCKWISE FROM BOTTOM RIGHT: A traditional bronze cleat fitted to the mainsheet of the 1939 classic yacht Zwerver.
Bollard cleats work well with larger lines which might jam on a conventional cleat.
The popular Clyde cleat designed by Davey & Co and found on many yachts from the 1930s.
Retractable cleats prevent the sheets getting tangled and save the crews' toes from getting stubbed.
The 100-year-old Herreshoff cleat is still going strong – albeit adapted here to fit around a fairlead.
A functional double bollard cleat welded to the bulwarks of a steel yacht.

It's a mark of the brilliance of the American designer Nat Herreshoff that not only are his boat designs still built and sold for hundreds of thousands of dollars, but the cleat he designed 100 years ago is not only replicated by dozens of manufacturers but is regarded as a piece of art. For, as well as being sold as a serious piece of sailing kit, the 6in (15cm) bronze Herreshoff cleat is also available as a pen set from Bristol Bronze for just $145, complete with two gold pens. Now that's an accolade.

The trick with Herreshoff's cleats was that they were hollow, making them lighter than comparable designs, and yet were designed in such a way that they were actually stronger than most solid cleats of the same size. And, as every yachtsman knows, strength and lightness make a

winning combination. Herreshoff's triumph didn't last long, however, as within a few decades the arrival of incredibly light yet strong cleats made of aluminium would completely supplant the use of bronze – and at a fraction of the price.

Back on the other side of the Atlantic, the British company Davey & Co started producing exquisite bronze fittings for yachts from 1885. Their range included the popular bar cleat (also known as a Clyde cleat), essentially a pair of bronze stanchions joined by a wooden bar, which is a feature of many classic British yachts. It's not known if the bar cleat has ever been made into a pen set, but Davey & Co do make their own version of the Herreshoff cleat, should the need arise.

FAIRLEADS

Time for a puzzle. What's being described here? 'It is an elegantly bowed aluminium device inside which two polyamide rollers rotate on stainless steel axles.' That is design jargon for a very common piece of kit: a fairlead. Admittedly it is a rather sophisticated fairlead designed for top-of-the-range yachts by German manufacturers Nomen (www. nomenproducts.de). But it gives you some idea of the pride that goes into designing even the simplest of yachting hardware.

Fairleads serve a simple purpose: to guide mooring lines over (or through) the bulwarks and prevent the lines chafing against them. At their simplest they might be two vertical pillars, such as those sported by many Victorian cutters, or they might incorporate rollers, rubbing plates and even cleat horns. The most common are made of a pair of rounded hooks facing each other, with a gap in the middle to receive the line. This simple formula has been replicated in hundreds of shapes and sizes and many different materials – although the most common materials are bronze, aluminium, galvanised steel and stainless steel. That's the one you're likely to see on 90% of yachts moored in a marina. We're still looking for Nomen's elegantly bowed fairlead with polyamide rollers…

1

3

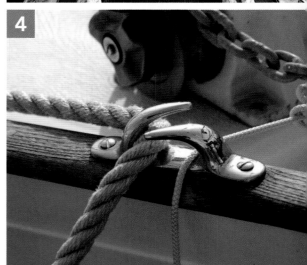

4

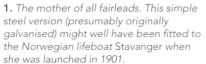

1. *The mother of all fairleads. This simple steel version (presumably originally galvanised) might well have been fitted to the Norwegian lifeboat Stavanger when she was launched in 1901.*
2. *On another level is this stainless steel double fairlead with rollers on the 1929 classic yacht Belle Aventure – though it's unlikely to be an original fitting.*

3. *A stemhead fitting with bling on this 1970s vintage yacht. The fairleads are doing their job nicely.*
4. *A stainless steel variation on the theme.*
5. *Built in 2003 to a 1939 design, Classic Addy is fitted with lookalike period fittings, including this fairlead.*
6. *A streamlined aluminium affair fitted to a modern production cruiser.*

SAMPSON POSTS

Long before boats had cleats they had sampson posts, and they are still in everyday use on many working boats and some yachts. Essentially a sturdy post sticking out of the foredeck, a traditional sampson (also spelled samson) post goes right through the deck and is attached to structural members such as the keelson. It's designed to be strong enough to take the weight of the whole boat while at anchor, when the chain (or 'rode') is transferred from the anchor winch to the post, and while being towed. Vessels not fitted with a sampson post are advised to tie the tow line to the base of the mast – the next strongest thing.

The modern interpretation of a sampson post is really just a stainless steel cleat bolted to the deck. It's not usually attached to any major structural members and shouldn't be relied on to take any more weight than you would put on a normal cleat – not without checking the fastening first, anyway. Most sampson posts nowadays have a bar through them for ease of tying off, but this makes it impossible to use any of the specialist knots that have evolved on workboats specially for the purpose. Knots such as the lighterman's (or tugboat) hitch, which can be simply wound around the post with one hand and a boot, if necessary, and untied just as easily even under tension. And who needs anything more complicated than that?

ABOVE: A sampson post fitted to the stern quarter of a fishing boat. Although the design is archaic, it's still in widespread use on working boats and some yachts.

OPPOSITE, TOP LEFT: A modern interpretation, neatly incorporated into the bowsprit fitting. In fact, this is really just a bollard cleat pretending to be a sampson post, as the fitting doesn't extend below decks.

OPPOSITE, TOP RIGHT: A proper, through-deck sampson post is put to good use on this wooden cruising yacht (though that bow line should be put in the fairlead before it chews a hole in the rail!). When at anchor, the chain is usually transferred from the winch to the post.

OPPOSITE, BOTTOM: This sampson post is doubling up as a bitt by holding the heel of the bowsprit. The idea is no doubt to keep the weight down on what is a very dainty bow. (Note the bowsprit whiskers and dolphin strikers, as discussed on p72.)

THE REAL DEAL

A traditional sampson post runs through the deck and the cabin sole, and is jointed to the keelson or other structural timber.

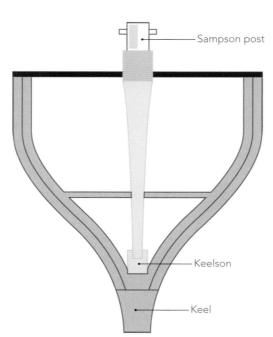

Sampson post

Keelson

Keel

BOW ROLLERS

1. *This bow roller holds the anchor snugly – possibly a bit too snugly, as the scratches on the side of the hull suggest it's not doing its job.*
2. *Retro-fitting bow rollers on a classic yacht is often problematic. This solution certainly preserves the original structure, though it's a bit of an eyesore.*
3. *A neat roller fitted on the bowsprit of a modern wooden cutter.*
4. *The enormous sheave on this sturdy roller ensures the Bruce anchor is held away from the hull.*
5. *Nothing but the best for this luxury yacht: double rollers and a stainless steel anchor.*
6. *The bow roller as style statement. This system certainly provides secure stowage for the anchor, but arguably detracts from the line of the boat.*
7. *A built-in roller on an aluminium hull – functional and not in the least ostentatious.*

There's only two things a bow roller needs to do: roll smoothly to minimise chafe from the anchor line or chain, and stop the anchor banging into the boat. Unfortunately, because there are so many types of anchors available, no bow roller can work perfectly for all of them, with the result that a boat often ends up with a mismatched combination.

There is one rule which applies to all bow rollers: the further out it sticks, the less likely the anchor is to cause damage to the bow. Which is why stubby mini-bowsprits are fitted to many yachts – not because the rig necessarily needs it, but because it's a good place to stow the anchor. The price you pay is aesthetics, as a protruding anchor makes a poor substitute for a traditional figurehead. For yachts already fitted with sail-carrying bowsprits, the challenge is to keep the bow roller as close to the centreline of the boat as possible without interfering with the bowsprit itself.

Despite its functional role, a bow roller can be a thing of beauty – whether it is made of wood, bronze or a dazzling display of stainless steel. Some might even be described as ostentatious, which certainly wasn't always the case.

ANCHORS

It used to be so simple. For centuries, the only anchor used by ships of any size was the Admiralty Pattern – the iconic one with two pointy bits (flukes) and a cross bar (stock), as drawn by every school child. Unless of course you were a Chinese, Indian or Viking school child, in which case you drew your own special type of anchor. The trouble with the Admiralty Pattern (also known as the fisherman) was that it was cumbersome and difficult to stow, particularly on large ships, so eventually a stockless version was invented which could be stowed flush against a ship's side.

Anchors intended specifically for yachts only really came into their own from 1933, when the British mathematician Geoffrey Ingram Taylor designed the CQR, based closely on the shape of a plough (hence its nickname). He was soon followed by American Richard Danforth, who in the 1940s invented an anchor consisting essentially of two giant flukes hinged to a shaft. Although the Danforth was designed to be used on landing craft, its compact shape soon made it popular among yachtsmen the world over. Since then, there's been an explosion of anchor designs, including the Bruce (a cross between a CQR and a Danforth), the Bulwagga (a Danforth with three flukes), the Rocna (an 'improved' CQR/Bruce) and the Hydrobubble (essentially a small plough fitted with a buoyancy tank).

Which one's best? Well, let's just say everyone's got their favourite.

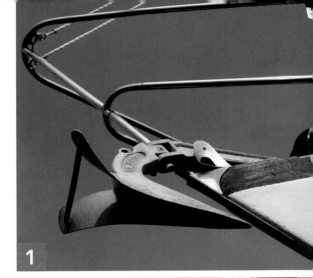

1. The iconic CQR, designed by a British mathematician in the 1930s and now available in multiple shapes and sizes.
2. An American Danforth anchor with an elaborate stowage system.
3. The CQR is awkward to stow on deck and needs custom-made chocks to hold it in place.
4. The Bügel anchor from Germany, which is widely available but lacks the sophistication of other anchors.
5. A Danforth in action, showing one of the limitations of the type: the line gets tangled around the stock (the perpendicular bar).
6. A Bruce anchor is lashed to the bows of this 1930s wooden yacht.

7. A stockless anchor, originally designed to stow flat against the sides of ships – though here resting on the deck of a small yacht.
8. The Admiralty Pattern anchor, and variations thereof, was ubiquitous aboard ships until the mid-1800s.
9. The original Bruce 'claw' anchor broke the mould when it was invented by Peter Bruce in the 1970s.
10. The Rocna (shown tucked up against the bowsprit of the 2009 pilot cutter Amelie Rose) is one of the most successful recent anchor designs.
11. The 1980s Delta is an improved CQR.

THIS PAGE: The stanchion and pulpit on this X-boat are the regulation 24in (600mm) height. The little nylon rollers protect the foresails from chafe.

OPPOSITE PAGE: The pulpit and stanchions are made of galvanised steel on this 1930s classic yacht.

GUARDRAILS & PULPITS

Guardrails on a boat seem like common sense: an essential safety device to prevent people falling overboard which no boat should be without. Yet it wasn't always thus. Right up until the 1960s, most yachts were built without

them and sailors relied on the principle of 'one hand for the boat, one hand for yourself' to keep them out of the briny. Indeed, there were some who thought guardrails made you lazy and less likely to take responsibility for your own safety, while others argued they were actually dangerous given they were usually at the perfect height to tip you head first into the sea. French sailing legend Bernard Moitessier sailed one-and-a-half times around the world without guardrails and was quoted as saying: 'It's better to learn to cling like a monkey.'

Nowadays, guardrails (or 'lifelines' in the USA) are mandatory in most offshore races, with strict regulations controlling their construction. Most racing authorities, such as the Royal Ocean Racing Club (RORC) which runs the Fastnet Race, insist on guardrails at least 24in (600mm) high on boats over 28ft long or 18in (450mm) for boats under 28ft, with stanchions no more than 7ft 2½in (2.2m) apart. More recently, and not without some controversy, the RORC has banned the use of high-modulus fibres such as Dyneema and Spectra for guardrails, insisting on uncovered stainless steel wire instead. Likewise, carbon fibre has been banned for stanchions and pulpits, which must also be of stainless steel. The new materials are not yet sufficiently proven, it seems, to be trusted with people's lives.

DAVITS

TOP LEFT: A traditional davit – essentially a bent steel pipe – is used to stow the anchor on this 1945 Greek fishing boat.

TOP RIGHT: Likewise the davits on this 1916 Maine windjammer. The span is greater here, however, and strengthening struts have been added to both davits. The dinghy is that quintessential American tender: the peapod.

Jeremy Rogers is best known as the builder of a line of successful yachts which dominated ocean racing in the 1970s and 1980s, including the ever popular Contessa 32 – which now numbers more than 650 and, 45 years later, is still in production. But boatbuilding no longer pays the bills for the famously pernickety craftsman: davit-building does. For, while Jeremy's boatbuilding business has been through several ups and downs, including bankruptcy in the 1980s, his davit-making business has gone from strength to strength, providing stylish carbon fibre davits for customers ranging from the Ministry of Defence and Trinity House to the growing band of superyacht owners. Davits, it seems, are big business.

Davits have been used on ships for centuries, for everything from hoisting groceries out of tenders to bringing anchors aboard ship, not forgetting their sometimes infamous role in lowering (or not lowering) lifeboats. At their simplest, they can be lengths of metal pipe bent into a suitable arc with a block and tackle attached to the end. At their most sophisticated they can be – well, like Jeremy's elegant Atlas davits.

The increasing popularity of RIBs as tenders on superyachts and even some cruising yachts is in part responsible for the explosion in demand for davits. They can also make a convenient dumping ground for much of today's essential cruising paraphernalia, such as solar panels, wind turbines, GPS aerials, etc, etc.

TOP LEFT: A hefty pair of davits are needed on the stern of the engineless schooner Mercantile to carry her yawl, a heavy motorised tender which is used to manoeuvre the ship in and out of harbour.

TOP RIGHT: Apart from the dinghy, the davits on this long-distance cruising yacht also carry solar panels, a danbuoy (safety device) and miscellaneous antennae and aerials.

FLAGS & FLAGSTAFFS

'Flag etiquette is a combination of law (what you must do) and maritime tradition (expectations of behaviour within the seafaring community). Being ill-informed of your obligations could lead you to cause insult at home or abroad by giving a signal you do not intend to give, or could lead you to a fine for breaking the law.' So says the website of the Royal Yachting Association (RYA), the UK's foremost sailing authority. It goes on to explain the order of seniority of flags' positions, namely: 1. The stern: Reserved for the ship's ensign. 2. Masthead: Reserved for the yacht's burgee (usually the yacht club it belongs to). 3. Starboard spreaders: Reserved for signalling and/or a courtesy flag (ie the flag of the country the ship is in, if cruising overseas). 4. Port spreaders: House flags, including membership of other clubs and associations, such as the RYA.

Traditions are liable to change, however, and as the yacht's masthead becomes increasingly cluttered up with navigation devices, burgees are moving down to the spreaders, with a knock-on effect on the other flags. Some yachts even fly two burgees on one halyard, a practice that might seem eminently practical but which would shock some die-hard traditionalists. As for the British national flag, it goes without saying that a union jack has no place aboard ship apart from on her jackstaff. Other than that, a red ensign should be used on all occasions, including as a courtesy flag on non-British yachts – unless you have special dispensation to fly a blue or white ensign. After all, manners maketh man.

TOP LEFT: Ship's ensigns denoting their country of registration are usually flown from a flagstaff at the stern – unless racing. This multinational line-up is at a Mediterranean classic yacht regatta.

BOTTOM LEFT: Ships dressed overall at a Tall Ships regatta in Scotland. It might look random, but there are recommended sequences, and both ships here have exactly the same flag order.

AMELIE ROSE'S FLAGS

As well as two 'house' flags, Amelie Rose flies a Breton and a French flag, presumably for Breton/French guests, a Celtic flag, a Dorset county flag, and various festival flags. It's not strictly 'etiquette', but it certainly looks festive.

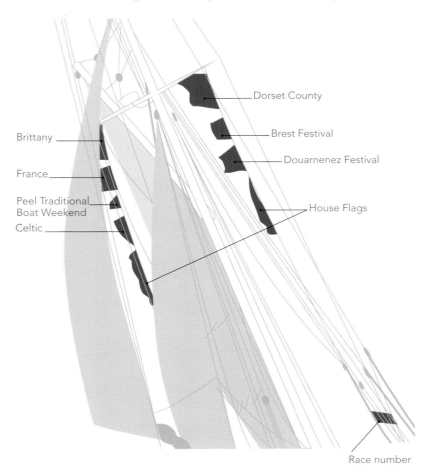

Dorset County

Brittany

Brest Festival

France

Douarnenez Festival

Peel Traditional
Boat Weekend

House Flags

Celtic

Race number

TOP RIGHT: Strictly speaking you don't need to fly a courtesy flag when you're visiting Scotland (yet!), but this classic yacht has one high up her mast – and it's almost as tall as her crew.

MIDDLE RIGHT, UPPER: The 2009 pilot cutter Amelie Rose racing on the Solent. She sported flags of many colours (see diagram), but no ensign – which is traditionally removed while racing.

MIDDLE RIGHT, LOWER: Some traditional sailing yachts fly an ensign from the corner of their mainsail while under way. These lateen-rigged Scout boats on the island of Spetses, in Greece, fly a Greek ensign or a local flag dating from the War of Independence.

BOTTOM RIGHT: No prizes for guessing what nationality these boats are. The event is a reunion of Sparkman & Stephens boats at Mystic Seaport, Connecticut.

PORTHOLES

Have you ever wondered why portholes are (usually) round? After all, houses have always managed with square windows, so why shouldn't boats do the same? The answer turns out to be not just a simple question of aesthetics or even superstition – square portholes are one of the few things not deemed to be unlucky aboard ship. No, it's just a matter of strength. Whereas a round frame might be said to actually strengthen a hull, a square window concentrates the stresses in the corners and weakens it. Not surprisingly, given the possible dire consequences of a porthole failing while at sea, builders tend to favour round frames. This is less of an issue in monocoque structures, such as fibreglass and composite hulls, where the stresses are more evenly distributed – which is why many modern yachts have square portholes.

Portholes were invented by a French boatbuilder, Descharges, in Brest, and were first fitted on Henry VIII's warship *Henry Grace à Dieu* in 1515. Early portholes were effectively square wooden ports which opened out to allow cannons to be fired. They allowed a second tier of cannon to be fitted below decks, without risk of letting in too much water in rough weather. They later developed their more domestic role of letting light and air into the ship and evolved into the iconic round portholes fitted to most vessels, until relatively recently. Descharges would no doubt be delighted to see that square portholes are back in fashion.

OPPOSITE: The classic bronze porthole, as fitted to ships and yachts for at least 100 years. This example has a bronze scoop under it to catch any drips – which has the drawback of rotting the neighbouring wood if not sponged out regularly.

BOTTOM LEFT: The modern equivalent: elongated to look more streamlined, with tinted glass and a simple frame. It has a certain minimalist beauty.

BOTTOM CENTRE: With the advent of strong homogeneous hulls, square and rectangular portholes and windows are fashionable once again – such as on this Bénéteau Océanis racer/cruiser.

BOTTOM RIGHT: As basic as it gets. A plain piece of Perspex is screwed onto the cabin side, with an off-the-shelf porthole let into its forward end. The chainplate in the foreground is built in a similar rudimentary style.

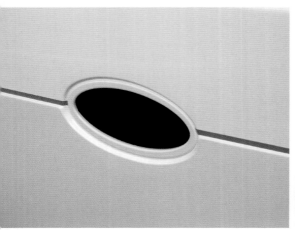

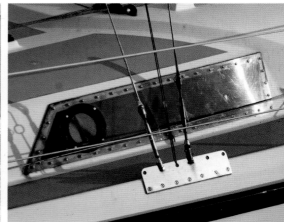

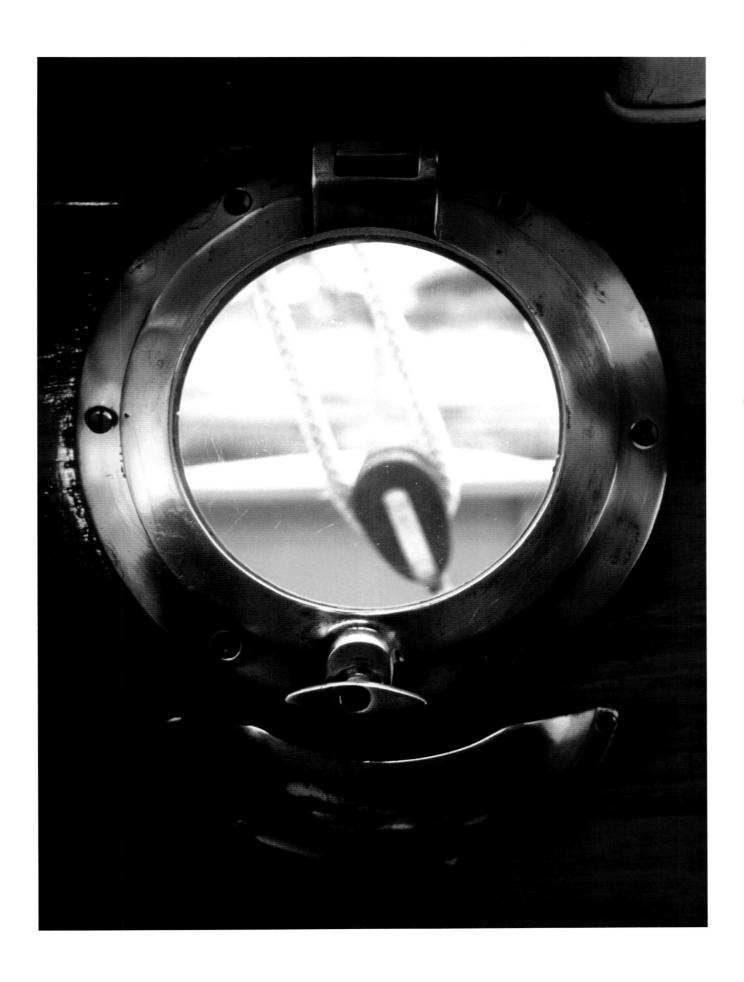

PASSERELLES & BOARDING LADDERS

There is something quintessentially Mediterranean about a passerelle. Whereas in most countries of the world, yachts either swing on a mooring or tie up to a floating dock, in the Med the tradition is to moor either bow or stern to the quay. Not only is this a challenge for newcomers not used to reversing into narrow spaces, but it also requires a passerelle to bridge the gap between yacht and quay. At its simplest, a passerelle can be a plank of wood – just like the gangplanks used to get aboard a ship when it's tied up alongside. At the other extreme are the carbon fibre gadgets which disappear into the back of a superyacht at the touch of a button and cost as much as a small yacht. Most yachts have something in between, usually made of wood and aluminium, held off the quay with a halyard, and fitted with a safety rail.

When not moored stern to or alongside, a boarding ladder can be used to get on and off ship – in fact, as the height of yachts' topsides has increased in recent years, a boarding ladder is now more necessary than ever. Many yachts make do with the ubiquitous detachable folding ladder, which works in most situations. But there's a lot to be said for a folding or telescopic ladder fitted to the transom which can be opened up should someone fall in the water when there's nobody else around. Better still, an open transom with swimming platform and built-in ladder can be a lifesaver.

TOP LEFT: A fine passerelle with removable teak gratings. The only things missing are railings and a halyard line to lift it off the jetty. Location? The Côte d'Azur, of course.

TOP RIGHT: Not everyone loves the modern 'sugar scoop' stern, but they do make getting on and off easier, particularly as yachts' sides ('freeboard') become ever-higher. This boarding/swimming ladder can be lowered with a flick of the rope.

BOTTOM LEFT: A boarding/swimming ladder fitted to the transom of an old-style cruising yacht.

BOTTOM RIGHT: This 50ft (15m) classic schooner takes a more utilitarian approach, with a simple plank of wood acting as a gangplank. Tellingly, this picture was taken in the Caribbean, not the Mediterranean.

VENTS

When it comes to vents, one name looms large: Dorade. The Dorade vent was designed by Olin Stephens – or more likely his younger and more 'practical' brother Rod – of the legendary yacht design company Sparkman & Stephens. It was a simple enough idea: a trumpet-shaped vent catches the wind and funnels it into a box attached to the yacht's deck or cabin top. From there, the draught flows into the yacht through a hole at the other end of the box. The clever bit is the raised lip (or baffle) around the hole, which prevents any errant water dripping into the boat. Instead, the water flows out through limber holes cut into the side of the box.

The fitting first appeared in 1929 on S&S's first major design, the two-times Fastnet winner *Dorade* – designed when Olin was just 21 – and featured on all subsequent S&S boats. The elements have been adapted since, with different shaped vents and all kinds of materials, but the basic principle remains the same.

A more primitive precursor to the Dorade vent is the mushroom vent: a rounded metal cap which screws down over a hole fitted with a raised lip to prevent water getting through. Modern variations combine a fixed round cowl located over a baffle with an electric fan powered by a small solar panel to increase ventilation. It's a lot neater than a Dorade vent, but probably a lot less efficient too.

OPPOSITE: The 1962 classic yacht Inward Bound *is bristling with period fittings, including lookalike Clyde cleats (see p122), substantial fairleads and a two-tier anchor windlass. The solar-powered fan vent (left) is, however, a modern addition.*

TOP LEFT: A traditional mushroom vent. The raised lip prevents water getting in when the vent is open, though the brass cowl should always be screwed down to close the fitting before going to sea.

TOP CENTRE: A fixed vent fitted to a Perspex hatch. Any water that gets into the vent is deflected by a baffle inside and flows out of the scuppers around its base.

TOP RIGHT: This modern rendition of the classic Dorade vent is on a Sparkman & Stephens daysailer launched in 2004 – exactly 75 years after the company invented the original fitting.

HOW IT WORKS

Any water that enters the vent escapes through scuppers, while fresh air rises over the baffle and makes its way below decks.

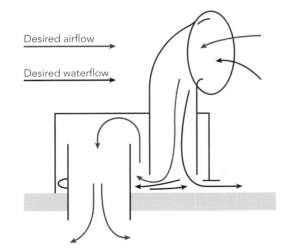

Desired airflow

Desired waterflow

LIFEBUOYS

They might sometimes look as if their only purpose is to have a yacht's name painted on them, but in an emergency they can mean the difference between life and death. Liferings (lifebuoys) have been fitted to vessels since the 1850s, when the classic O-ring was invented by Royal Navy officer Lt Thomas Kisbee. Cork was the standard material for most early liferings, sometimes (and controversially) substituted with kapok fibre, even though it was flammable and had a tendency to become saturated. Even now the UK's Maritime & Coastguard Agency uses cork, or 'other equally efficient buoyant material', as the standard. It also states that a lifebuoy 'shall not be filled with rushes, cork shavings, granulated cork or any other loose granulated material' and that it should be able to float in fresh water for 24 hours with a 40lb (14.5kg) iron weight attached.

Nowadays, horseshoe buoys are more popular than the traditional ring, and they do have a more purposeful air, particularly when attached to a light and a danbuoy (another obligatory piece of safety equipment in many of today's races). And cork has long since been replaced with synthetic materials such as polystyrene and polyurethane. Either way, the boat's name should still be painted on the buoy, as required by the Maritime & Coastguard Agency – not for decorative purposes, but for identification in case the boat sinks.

ABOVE: A pair of liferings are casually looped around the aft sampson posts of the 1888 classic yacht Bonita. Note the lack of guardrails, appropriate to a yacht of her era.

OPPOSITE, CLOCKWISE FROM TOP LEFT: The danbuoy and horseshoe lifebuoy are well located for immediate deployment on this 2006 cruiser/racer. The traditional liferings on these classic yachts might look purely decorative, but they are genuine modern lifesaving gear which can save life in an emergency. A variation on the horseshoe theme, described by the manufacturers as 'simply indestructible', though it looks like it might also be distinctly uncomfortable to wear. These yachts moored up in northern Poland are fitted with ample lifebuoys.

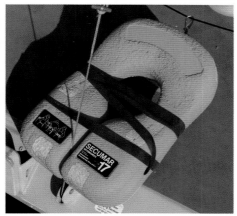

CHAFE GUARDS

Anyone who's owned a boat will be aware of the dangers of chafe. A mooring line left on an exposed rail can chafe a deep gouge in the surface in a matter of days – and there's usually no way you can fix that without some major surgery. Which is why rubbing strips have been a feature of boats probably for as long as boats and ropes have co-existed. The traditional method is to tack a sheet of copper or to screw brass strips over the affected area – which is usually the top of the bulwarks where mooring lines and running rigging rest. Strips of wood, such as oak or teak, can be applied in the same way, particularly to the spars.

On modern yachts, copper and brass have been replaced with stainless steel, which is usually more in keeping with the rest of the vessel's hardware. To simplify things even further, self-adhesive strips of stainless steel are now available which can be fitted without having to drill holes for screws. At 0.5mm thick, these are thin enough that they can be bent around a vulnerable corner, in the same way as the copper sheets of old. What's good for the goose is good for the gander, and mooring lines can also be protected from chafe using lengths of rubber hose or specially designed nylon sleeves with Velcro seams.

OPPOSITE, TOP: You don't want your irreplaceable classic yacht worn away by capricious mooring lines, which is why the stern of the 1957 ketch Lone Fox is protected by a hefty strip of stainless steel.

OPPOSITE, BOTTOM: The need for these brass strips isn't immediately obvious, but once the sail is raised and the mainsheet eased out, the boom is likely to chafe against the wire rigging. And you don't want to scratch the varnish on a 1930s classic such as Lulworth.

BOTTOM LEFT: The modern equivalent: a stainless steel strip screwed to the toe rail of a modern production cruiser.

BOTTOM CENTRE: Chafe guards can be beautiful, as demonstrated by the copper plate on the 1945 Greek caique Faneromeni.

BOTTOM RIGHT: An alternative is to slide some plastic hose over the offending lines – though it looks as if it might be a little late for this boat.

ROPEWORK

The image of the ancient mariner busying himself tying fancy knots as his ship tears around the oceans of the world has become something of a cliché. Decorative knots are still very much in use though, and not just as coasters and doormats. True they are mostly found on traditional yachts, but there's no reason why they shouldn't be used on modern yachts too. The classic place to tie a decorative knot is on the tiller, where it not only prevents a wooden tiller splitting but also stops the hand slipping off the end. A plain Turk's head is usually used or, if more grip is needed, some other fancy knotwork such as coachwhipping or a continuous wall hitch. All can be applied to traditional and modern tillers alike.

Another common use of decorative knots is for mats, either at the foot of the gangplank or as a 'thump mat' under deck-mounted blocks to prevent banging and chaffing. A flat Turk's head is ideal for the purpose, while making an ocean plait mat is an adventure in itself. Again, there's no reason why this shouldn't be done on a modern fibreglass yacht, although many deck-mounted blocks are now fitted with spring collars to prevent them falling over. Other common applications for knots are ratlines, bowsprit nets, railing chafe pads (that Turk's head again) and of course that old favourite: the bell rope. Get knotting!

ABOVE: Ropework at the end of a tiller not only looks good, but protects the wood and provides better grip. From left to right: a Turk's head, coachwhipping, another Turk's head, continuous wall knot, and another Turk's head.

OPPOSITE, TOP: The skill in making a bowsprit net like this isn't in tying the knots, but planning the design and keeping the tension even.

BOTTOM LEFT: A flat Turk's head makes a perfect 'thump mat' to stop a block (not shown in this picture) banging against the deck.

BOTTOM RIGHT: A simple rope 'whipping' around this mast traveller protects the varnish on this lug-rigged dinghy.

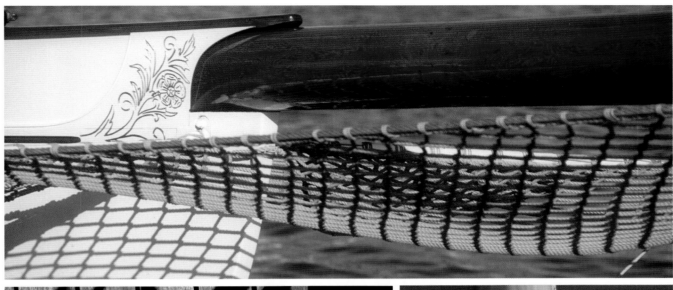

LEATHERWORK

Another traditional material with a modern application is leather. Animal hide has been used on boats as protection against chafe for hundreds of years and is still used on modern yachts, often combined with the latest technology. For, as anyone who has tried to buy non-leather shoes knows, no manmade material is quite as good as leather, in terms of looks, durability and feel. Which is why you have the surprising sight of state-of-the-art Kevlar blocks wrapped in protective leather, carbon fibre spinnaker poles with leather rubbing strips, and cool stainless steel wheels encased in leather jackets – after all, who wants to hold a cold metal helm on a frosty early morning sail?

Although leather covers are usually stitched together, strips of leather can also be placed over larger areas and tacked into place, not unlike copper and stainless steel sheets, which is useful for such items as boom gallows, gaff jaws and spars. Leather chafe pads can also be glued in place using contact glue – though the self-adhesive leather pad has yet to be invented.

Historically, leather played an even greater role in maritime affairs, and was used for everything from sails to snorkels and even hull coverings – including the world's first submarine. The Irish curraghs were covered in leather right up until the last century and were capable of crossing oceans – as demonstrated by Tim Severin during his famous St Brendan voyage. It's only a matter of time before someone builds a carbon fibre curragh covered in leather…

LEFT: Stitching a leather boot to the mizzen mast of the 1909 classic yacht Owl.

OPPOSITE PAGE, CLOCKWISE FROM TOP LEFT: Leather covers have been stitched over the guardrail attachments on this modern yacht – more likely to protect the sails than out of consideration for its crew.
This spinnaker halyard has a leather cover to prevent the thin sail material snagging.
The large genoa on this classic yacht is pulled tight against the rigging terminals (see p60) – without the leather covers, the sail would tear or get covered in grease.
The shackle joining the rigging to a block is covered to protect the mainsail of this classic yacht.
Copper tacks can also be used to attach the leather strips, as shown on the gaff jaw of this traditional dinghy.
The shackle under this block is out of reach of the sail, but might catch the crews' toes if it wasn't covered.

FENDERS

There's certainly nothing very glamorous about fenders and neither are they very photogenic, but they do form an essential part of a yacht's inventory. Without fenders, the boat's topsides would chafe against every harbour wall and every other vessel's topsides – and the kids wouldn't have ready-made floats for their rafts. There was a time when moderately glamorous and quite photogenic fenders were crafted out of rope, but these were heavy when wet and almost as unyielding as the topsides they were meant to protect. They are now only used by die-hard traditionalists and on narrowboats. Modern yacht fenders are made from rubber, foam or plastic and come in many shapes and sizes, depending on the size of boat and where they are being used. They can even be colour-coded to match the yacht's colour scheme.

The most controversial issue about fenders though is not how unphotogenic they are but what knot to tie them with and where. Walk into any marina, and the majority of fenders will be tied to the lifeline with a clove hitch knot. This is a double sin as not only can they slide up and down the lifeline but they are likely to come undone altogether as the clove hitch is not a secure knot. Much better to tie the fenders to the stanchions themselves or some other strong point using a secure knot such as a round turn and two half hitches, or possibly a spar hitch, a more secure variant of the clove hitch. You have been warned!

1. *Colour coordinated fenders! But have they been tied to the boat correctly, in other words with a round turn and two half hitches?*
2. *Another issue with fenders is what to do with them when they are not in use. Here's one neat solution.*
3. *Why have fenders on the 'outer' side of the boat? In case another boat bumps into you, of course!*

4. *A purpose-made bow fender, or bow protector.*
5. *It's not pretty, but a large round fender is a useful precaution, especially while manoeuvring.*
6. *Traditional fenders are made of rope and filled with a variety of substances, including horsehair and cork.*

1

4

2

3

5

6

AWNINGS & COVERS

There was a time when canvas covers protected the boat; now, increasingly, awnings and suchlike are used to protect the people who sail them. Back in the 1920s and 1930s, traditional wooden hatches had a tendency to leak and the yachts themselves were more susceptible to wear and tear, so it made sense to fit covers on anything which was likely to leak or become mushy. Nowadays, hatches are less leaky and a yacht's whole fabric is more durable, so there's less need to cover everything. Humans, on the other hand, seem less able to cope with the elements, so most yachts are now fitted with sprayhoods, which protect the cockpit crew from spray, and an assortment of awnings, canopies and wind chutes to protect them from the heat. Most delightful of all is the bimini, which is essentially a lightweight awning stretched between two poles. But whereas an awning suggests something rather durable and earnest, a bimini immediately conveys the idea of sandy beaches, turquoise waters and cocktails – in short, the Bahamas.

Boat covers may be making a comeback, however. For while high-tech materials such as carbon fibre and Kevlar may be immeasurably lighter and stronger than their traditional counterparts, they are proving less resistant to ultraviolet rays from the sun, prompting a resurgence of covers on wheels and other susceptible parts.

ABOVE: If you haven't got a wheelhouse, a simple sprayhood such as this makes all the difference when sailing through rough seas.

OPPOSITE PAGE, TOP: The semi-permanent aft awning on the 1910 classic yacht Eveline suggests she's based somewhere with a hot climate. Or, to be more precise, Malaysia.

BOTTOM LEFT: Covers are coming back into fashion on racing yachts made of expensive modern materials, such as carbon fibre and Kevlar, which degrade in the sun.

BOTTOM RIGHT: A good winter cover can reduce maintenance dramatically and extend the life of an old boat by decades. Just make sure there's plenty of ventilation too.

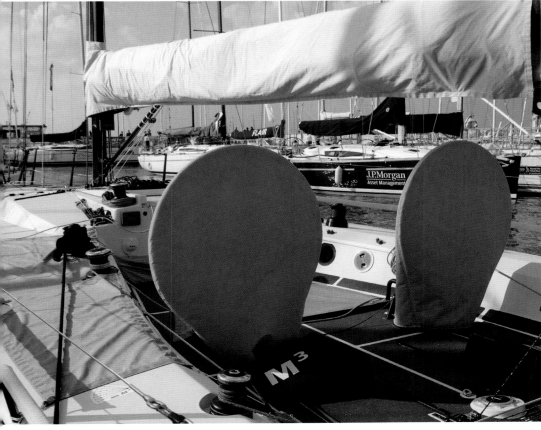

TENDERS

There are few topics that cause as much heartache to the average yachtsman as choosing a tender. The fundamental problem is that tenders are required to do too many things: carry heavy loads between ship and shore, lay an anchor, take crews on expeditions to unknown parts, carry boat maintenance crews around the mother ship, take the kids waterskiing and, in extremis, act as a lifeboat. They've also got to stow easily, either in a locker, on deck or on davits. And they should be able to be powered by sail, oar, and outboard.

It's a tall order for any boat to fulfil all these requirements, and most are better at some things than others. Tenders fall into four broad categories. There are inflatable dinghies, which perform poorly under sail, oar and outboard, but can be easily stowed. There are solid dinghies, which perform well under sail, oar and outboard, but are difficult to stow. There are RIBs (Rigid Inflatable Boats), which perform poorly under sail and oar and are difficult to stow, but are brilliant under outboard. Then there are stacking dinghies, folding dinghies and canvas dinghies, all of which have their own devout following.

The most popular? The inflatable dinghy, by far. It's the worst all rounder but can usually be stowed in a cockpit locker and is generally cheaper than its solid counterparts. Unless you own a superyacht, of course, in which case a RIB is *de rigeur*.

OPPOSITE PAGE, TOP LEFT: A pretty homebuilt pram dinghy (ie it doesn't have a 'pointy' bow) in the D'Entrecasteaux Channel, Tasmania.

TOP RIGHT: A simple dinghy like this gives the kids unimaginable freedom – though it's a tad too small to be a good tender.

BOTTOM LEFT: An exquisitely built clinker ply dinghy, which would grace the deck of any large yacht – but is too big for most.

BOTTOM RIGHT: The default inflatable dinghy that most yachts end up with, rigged here with a downwind sail for a 'flubber' race.

THIS PAGE, BELOW LEFT: A traditional clinker-built dinghy by UK boatbuilder Ashley Butler, taking Bumkin the cat for his constitutional.

BELOW RIGHT: Caribbean cruising legend Don Street at the oars of his tiny clinker pram, which fits comfortably on the deck of his 1905 yacht Iolaire.

6

BELOW
DECKS

It's an often overlooked fact that it takes twice as long to fit out the interior of a yacht as it does to build the hull and deck. That's because, unlike a house, nothing is ever straight or square, and most things are angled or curved in two directions at once. It's a joiner's worst nightmare, but it also produces exceptional interiors built to a high standard of craftsmanship. This chapter examines some of the questions which influence a yacht's interior design. Such as what size should your chart table be? Which way should your bunks face? Why should an icebox open from the top? And which are the best-loved heads?

SALOONS

Salon or saloon? Call me old-fashioned, but I'm going to hold out for tradition here. The term 'saloon' may have been tainted by its association with 'saloon bars', but it's the name that's been used to describe the lounge area of ships by English-speaking sailors for the past few centuries, and it seems a shame to lose that connection for the sake of a few sanitised sales brochures. A salon is a reception room in France, or somewhere people have their hair cut; the communal area of a sailing yacht is a saloon.

Aside from the issue of terminology, there are many other important considerations when designing a yacht's saloon: the number of seats/berths, the position of the table, seat height, storage, lighting, ventilation, heating, etc. The traditional solution is to have a pair of fore-and-aft settee bunks with a table between them, with some mechanism to turn one of the settees into a double berth. More hard-working boats opt for pilot bunks behind the settees, which works well on longer passages and while racing but excludes the option of a double berth. For those in colder climes there's the added complication of heating. A solid fuel stove? A diesel or paraffin heater mounted to a bulkhead? It's a bit like a jigsaw puzzle really, but in 3D.

TOP LEFT: A compact saloon on a 25ft (8m) yacht, with a full-length bunk on either side, chart table on the left and galley on the right. A table swings round and folds from around the corner on the right.

TOP RIGHT: A woodburning stove is a fine addition to a boat, but you need space to store the fuel.

MIDDLE LEFT: A sensible saloon on the traditionally styled Contessa 32 cruising yacht. An infill converts the bunk on the left (port side) to a double bed.

MIDDLE RIGHT: Pilot berths are an excellent option on a larger yacht, but significantly reduce the overall width of the saloon.

BOTTOM LEFT: The backs of the seats of this modern classic yacht hinge up and turn into bunks – replicating the interior of the famous Concordia Yawl.

BOTTOM RIGHT: A neat, triple leaf table, with a pair of lounging seats on either side instead of a bunk.

SALOON ERGONOMICS

There are many considerations to bear in mind when designing a yacht – not least the ergonomics of the space. Too much space can be as dangerous as too little, as the crew need to brace themselves in a seaway.

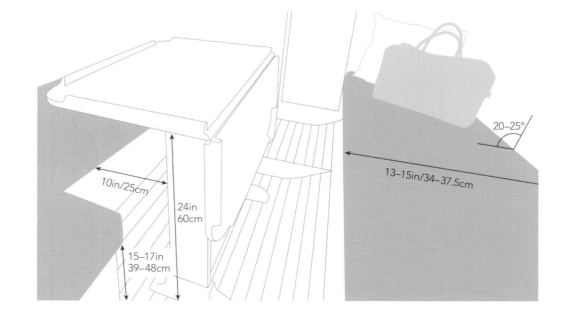

10in/25cm

24in 60cm

15–17in 39–48cm

20–25°

13–15in/34–37.5cm

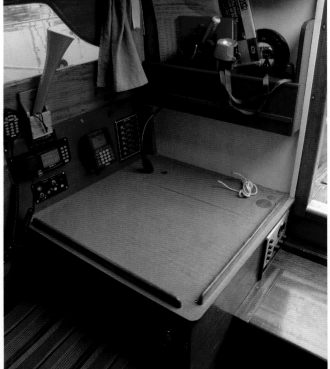

CHART TABLES

Given that the standard size for an Admiralty chart is about 40 x 28in (they do vary), you might imagine all yachts would be fitted with chart tables as big as that or bigger. In practice, finding that much space on a small boat is almost impossible, and most people usually settle for something big enough to take an Admiralty chart folded in two. The Admiralty itself has taken this on board, and produced a range of leisure charts which are A2 size (ie 23.4 x 16.5in/ 594 x 420mm), while most other chart manufacturers have long ago embraced smaller charts. That said, if there's space for a full-size chart table, it's always the best option.

With the advent of digital charts, in the form of chartplotters and computer programs, a chart table might seem increasingly redundant. In fact, the new technology seems to have had the opposite effect, as sailors tend to use both mediums. A well-designed chart table therefore needs to accommodate a paper chart and a laptop, perhaps on a retractable shelf. Then there is all the navigation paraphernalia, such as dividers, parallel rules, pencils and log book, not to mention log, depth sounder, GPS, VHF and all the other essential gear.

TOP: A luxury chart table on the 1924 classic yacht Astor. The only trouble here is that everything is likely to go flying off at the first big wave.

BOTTOM LEFT: A modern (and very ugly) alternative on a Lagoon catamaran. This chart table can only take a chart folded in four.

BOTTOM CENTRE: A compact chart table on a 1960s pocket cruiser, complete with period Formica. The 'fiddles' stop things rolling off, but also get in the way when navigating.

BOTTOM RIGHT: A more ergonomic chart table, with a rounded corner and fiddle on one side. The small Folio chart fits comfortably, and even a full-size chart might just squeeze on.

GALLEYS

Everyone knows a steady supply of comforting food, including regular hot meals, is the secret to a happy crew. Which is why it's strange that so many boats are fitted with inadequate galleys. It's not all about size – in fact, a compact galley which the crew can wedge themselves in while at sea is often better than a long, open galley with no bracing points. And, while it's generally accepted the best place for a galley is near the middle of the boat where there is least motion and near a companionway to provide fresh air, there are plenty of yacht designers willing to ignore these basic rules.

What it's really about are the countless details. Where possible, sinks should be near the centreline of the boat, rather than on the side, so that they can drain properly on both tacks. Likewise, the stove should preferably be facing forwards or aft, so if there is any spillage due to the boat rolling it's less likely to fall on the cook. If the stove is fitted sideways, it should be gimballed to reduce the risk of injury. The work surfaces should be fitted with strong fiddles at least 1in (25mm) high to prevent anything falling off while at sea, but leave the corners open to make cleaning easier. The icebox should open from the top rather than the side, to stop the cold air pouring out every time you use it. And so it goes on. A seaworthy galley is a mighty fine thing indeed.

ABOVE: The galley of a Contessa 32, with Corian worktop and gimballed stove. All that's missing is a belt for the crew to strap themselves in with.

OPPOSITE PAGE, TOP: The elegant oak galley of the 47ft (14.5m) classic yacht Owl. Even on a boat of this size, however, the sink is awkwardly positioned and workspace is in short supply.

LEFT: Built in 1860, the gaff yawl Cleone can be forgiven for not having the most luxurious galley in the world.

UPPER RIGHT: Handles fitted to the fridge of the 1931 Sparkman & Stephens training schooner Brilliant.

LOWER RIGHT: Brass and oak feature heavily in the interior of the replica classic yacht Integrity, built in 2012 by Stirling & Son.

CABINS

Cabins are another area where size isn't everything. A wide bunk might feel very luxurious when you're moored up in the marina, but once the boat is under way and you're being tossed from one side of the bunk to the other, you'll wish you'd chosen the narrow berth. A width of 24 inches is just about right – about two-thirds the width of a typical single bed. Lee boards or lee cloths are essential to stop you rolling out of bed – or at least worrying about rolling out of bed. And if you are lucky enough to have space for a permanent double bunk, then make sure the mattress is made in two halves so you can rig a lee cloth down the middle while at sea.

Cabins should have sufficient storage space for each crew member to have their own drawer and hanging area. And drawers should have strong latches or lift-up stops to prevent them opening in rough weather. Oh, and it goes without saying that bunks should be orientated fore-and-aft, not transversely across the beam – no one likes waking up with a rush of blood to the head when the boat changes tack.

OPPOSITE PAGE, TOP: For luxury like this, you'll have to save up for a 150ft (46m) classic yacht such as Lulworth – or you can charter her for 60,000 Euros a week.

BOTTOM LEFT: A nice shell motif on the oak drawers of the 1909 classic yacht Owl.

BOTTOM RIGHT: Twin berths in the bows of this modern cruising yacht make the most of what could be an awkward space. An infill turns them into a double bunk, with optional lee cloths in between.

HEADS

OPPOSITE PAGE, LEFT: *The Contessa 32 has a manual heads, with a sliding sink which pulls out over it. The shower drains out through the teak grating visible bottom left, into a 'grey water' tank.*

RIGHT: *A perfect place to spend a quiet moment...the heads on the replica cutter* Integrity, *complete with a refurbished Victory toilet from Blake's. Note the central bowsprit bitt, which runs through the deck right down to the keelson (see p74).*

BOTTOM LEFT: *A hand-operated water pump on the mini gentleman's yacht* Lyra.

BOTTOM RIGHT: *Plenty of space on this 45ft (13.7m) barge yacht for a generous shower room with house-like fittings.*

There was a time when sailing was such a minority sport that sailors could quite happily pump their effluent straight into the sea, safe in the knowledge that all they were doing was providing the local fish with a free meal. That's no longer the case, and many countries now insist that yachts are fitted with 'black water' tanks to collect toilet waste until it can be safely pumped out in a marina. Although this is mostly done on a voluntary basis in the EU, yachtsmen in the USA can be fined $2,000 for not having the right equipment. Fitting holding tanks on a large yacht is a simple if costly exercise, but it can be extremely problematic on anything under 30ft. Chemical toilets are often the answer, although they come with their own set of issues, not least of which is smell.

The quintessential yacht's heads are those produced by Blake & Son, a British company founded in 1798 which made its name with compact, reliable heads such as the Blakes Victory and the Blakes Baby. Both varieties are still in production, 75 years after they were first made, and the company still offers a comprehensive spare parts and repair service (including repainting) for all its vintage heads. Now that's what I call service.

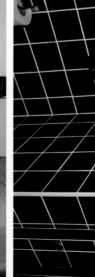

CHAPTER

7 MECHANICS

For those who have heard the 'wild call', it's tempting to put to sea with just 'a tall ship and a star to steer her by', like the hero of John Masefield's poem *Sea Fever*. For most of us, however, reality intrudes in the form of compasses, navigation lights, engines and the necessity of being back in the office on Monday morning. Happily, much of this boat gear is beautiful in its own right and deserving of some detailed photography. Who could resist that antique Wilfrid O White compass? Or almost any of the long line of Simpson Lawrence anchor windlasses? Or even that lovely shiny Volvo folding propeller?

 # ENGINES

It's an almost universal rule that speed boats are fitted with petrol engines, while sailboats and more sluggish motor yachts have diesel engines. Petrol (or 'gas' in US parlance) is said to be more flammable than diesel, while diesel engines are regarded as more reliable and longer-lasting. Recent research suggests this is all bunkum. Sure, if you're going to motor a large vessel at low speeds for days on end, a heavy old diesel engine will consume less fuel and suffer less wear and tear. For the average sailor, mostly nipping in and out of a marina on their 30ft (9m) yacht, a petrol engine will do the job very well, and at a fraction of the price.

Still, you can't mess with people's prejudices, and most of the engines shown on these pages are diesel, as are most engines fitted in most small sailing yachts. Even the handsome eco engine from Hybrid Marine in the UK is made up of an electric engine which 'piggybacks' a diesel engine – and diesel does emit less CO_2 than petrol. The clever part about this engine is that, by 'locking' the propeller shaft while under sail, the electric engine turns into a generator which recharges the batteries. Unlock the shaft, and you can motor into harbour using the power you've just generated, without emitting any CO_2 at all. Petrol or diesel? In future, the answer will almost always be 'electric'.

TOP LEFT: A typical diesel engine fitted, in this case, on a large steel cruising yacht. Most sailors prefer diesel, although petrol is as efficient and considerably cheaper.

TOP MIDDLE: An outboard is a sensible option on a small yacht such as this pocket cruiser, although it puts extra weight in the stern where you don't want it.

TOP RIGHT: This electric engine 'piggybacks' the diesel engine in the background and acts as a generator when the yacht is sailing.

OPPOSITE PAGE: Kelvin diesel engines were the dependable workhorses of fishing boats around the world for most of the 21st century. This 112hp beast was fitted to the Greek caique Faneromeni in 1972 and is still going strong.

PROPELLERS

There's no question that the most efficient type of propeller for motoring is the fixed, three (or more) bladed variety. Trouble is, once under sail, that prop creates a phenomenal amount of drag and will slow a small boat down by up to 1 knot. That might not sound like much, but it can add hours to a short crossing, and days or even weeks to a longer voyage. It's a conundrum that's perplexed designers since at least 1839, when the first propeller-driven steamship was built with a retractable prop to reduce drag. The ship was called the SS *Archimedes*, in honour of the Greek mathematician who invented the Archimedes screw, the concept behind all propellers.

One solution to the problem of drag, in the days when most yachts had long keels, was to fit a two-bladed prop and line it up with the keel while sailing. Modern fin keels and skeg rudders don't provide such a neat hiding place, however, so other solutions had to be found. Most efficient is a folding prop, which simply folds away when not in use – the two-bladed versions are the most streamlined, while the three-bladed versions perform better under power. Another route is feathering props, where the blades rotate to present the least drag under sail. Feathering props are slightly less efficient than folding props under sail, but are generally better under power. The only catch with both these inventions is price: either one will cost several times the price of a fixed three-bladed prop. But then, what price speed?

MEASURING THE PITCH

Pitch is the theoretical distance a propeller travels through water during a single rotation

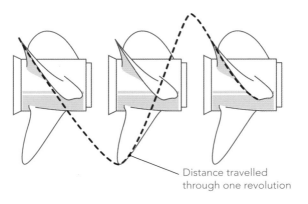

Distance travelled through one revolution

OPPOSITE: The 131ft (40m) schooner Coronet *displays her traditional (but non-original) three-bladed props. The engines and propellers have since been removed to return her to her original 1885 form.*

BELOW LEFT: Bow-thrusters are becoming more common on sailing yachts that need to manoeuvre into tight spaces.

BELOW CENTRE: The Volvo three-bladed folding propeller is said to provide as much speed or more as a fixed prop.

BELOW RIGHT: The skeg of a saildrive propeller sticks out vertically from the bottom of the boat, like the bottom part of an outboard, which suits the shape of some modern boats better.

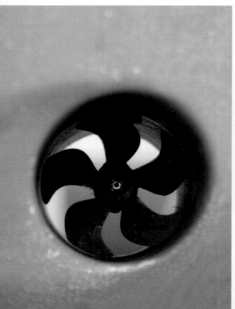

WINDLASSES

TOP LEFT: Vertical windlasses, such as the Sprint 1000 from Simpson-Lawrence, are increasingly popular on modern yachts. This one has a gypsy (or 'wildcat') for chain and a drum for rope, and is operated by an electric motor fitted under the deck.

TOP RIGHT: A traditional horizontal yacht windlass. Both the drum (left) and the gypsy (right) are operated by a long handle which fits into the uppermost lever.

The names say it all. Sea Wolf, Sea Tiger, Atlas, Royal, Prince, Duke, Regal, Anchormax, Anchorman… These names are all designed to inspire confidence, to appear solid and reliable. For if there's one thing you don't want breaking down when you're heading out from an exposed bay to avoid an incoming storm, it's the windlass. Which is why for the past 2,000 years sailors have experimented with different types of chain-hauling equipment. Historically, the most common was a windlass with a horizontal shaft, with a gypsy (or wildcat in the USA) on one side for the anchor chain, and a warping head (or drum) on the other side for mooring lines. This was, and still is, incorporated into the bits (the posts which run through the deck to the keelson and hold the inboard end of the bowsprit – see page 74). Or it could be bought off the shelf as a freestanding unit

and powered either by electricity, hydraulics, hand or, in some cases, foot.

Despite all the advantages of the horizontal windlass, however, it takes up a lot of deck space and provides an automatic tripping point for errant jib sheets – not to mention crews' feet and legs. The modern preference is therefore for a vertical windlass (strictly speaking called a capstan), where the mechanics are mostly located below decks. This can be fitted with just a gypsy and tucked away in a recess in the deck, or with a gypsy and a warp drum, where the drum usually protrudes above deck level. Powered by electricity or by hand, they have made the task of raising the anchor much more straightforward – though names such as Project 1000, CPX 2, VS1000 and RC-8 have lost some of the magic of their predecessors.

TOP LEFT: This more recent Sprint 1000 is fitted with a gypsy that is suitable for rope and chain. The sleek design is a big advance on traditional winches, although it is dependent on having a good supply of electricity.

TOP RIGHT: A traditional hydraulic winch fitted to the 1915 Baltic trader Circe. It might look over-elaborate, but bear in mind it was built to lift the two anchors of a 51-ton ship – something the Sprint 1000 would blow a fuse if asked to do.

NAVIGATION INSTRUMENTS

There was an appealing simplicity to the navigation instruments carried by most yachts at the beginning of the last century. A magnetic compass told you what course you were on; a log told you how far you'd travelled over the water (and therefore how fast you were going); a lead line told you how much water was under your boat; and a tell tale (piece of thread) on the rigging told you where the wind was coming from. If you were travelling out of sight of land, a sextant gave you your position, which you marked on a paper chart.

Gradually, things got more complicated. Paddlewheel logs replaced the trailing log, echo sounders replaced the lead line, and GPS replaced just about everything else. But the most dramatic change in today's navigation instruments is their ability to 'talk' to each other via a computer as part of an integrated system. Thus the wind instrument can talk to the speed instrument and work out the true wind direction (rather than apparent), the speed made to windward, and even your optimum heading on the next tack. Plug in your GPS, and it will calculate tidal drift and leeway and give you a course heading which takes into account all the prevailing conditions. All you have to do now is connect up your autopilot and you can put your feet up and let the computer sail the boat. Cocktails anyone?

OPPOSITE, ABOVE: An integrated system such as this, on board the Open 60 racing yacht Hugo Boss, allows instruments to 'talk' to one another and give a more accurate picture of what's going on.

BOTTOM LEFT: A classic Walker's log. A spinner attached to a line is towed behind the boat and turns the counter, giving the distance travelled over water – simple but effective.

BOTTOM CENTRE: Digital charts are increasingly popular, even on traditional boats such as the 1895 Norwegian rescue ship Christiania – though most still carry paper versions below decks.

BOTTOM RIGHT: The Volvo Ocean Race boats were fitted with powerful telecommunication systems which allowed images and video clips of the race to be broadcast around the world.

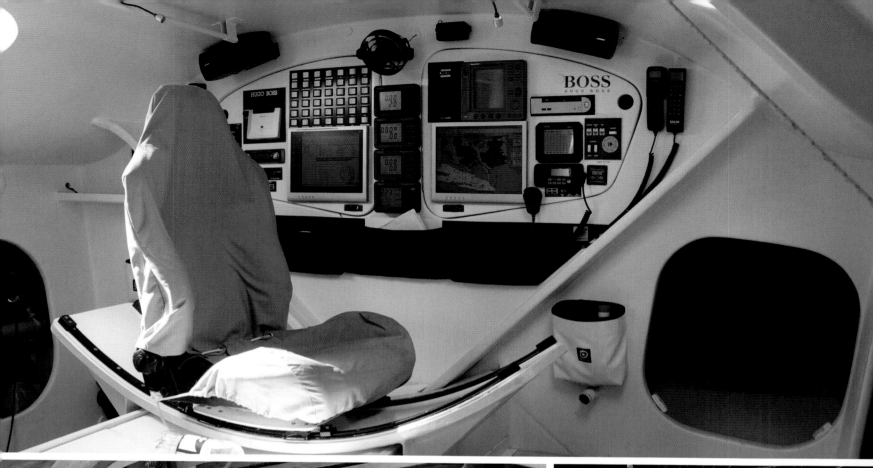

COMPASSES

Despite many attempts to invent all kinds of fancy replacements, the compass of choice on most yachts is still the magnetic compass – the same type of compass that's been used for navigation for at least 3,000 years. Sure, the design and materials might have changed, but the concept of using magnets to align a needle or card with the earth's magnetic field remains the same. And, while digital compasses have been available for several years, there's an intuitive process involved in using a magnetic compass which is much more closely connected to the physical experience of sailing a boat.

Since all magnetic compasses work the same way, for most yachtsmen

TOP LEFT: The classic Sestrel Moore compass was the default instrument of choice for many ocean-going yachts during the mid-1900s.

MIDDLE LEFT: The six lubber lines of this Venus compass allow the course to be read from different positions and can be used to estimate the position of other objects relative to the boat (eg landmarks and buoys).

BOTTOM LEFT: The Wilfred O White Company has been producing compasses like this for the past 100 years. This one is on the 1932 schooner Brilliant.

BOTTOM RIGHT: A modern mass-produced compass from brand leader Plastimo. Three lumber lines are provided so the course can be read while motoring (central) or while on either tack (on each side).

it's simply a choice of what shape compass to buy. Larger vessels, which are frequently helmed standing up or from a raised seat, often have flat card compasses, held in a binnacle, with the lubber line (the line used to read the bearing) on the forward side of the card. This is the classic set-up seen on any number of pirate ship movies. Modern yachts tend to have smaller compasses with cylindrical or even conical cards. These can be recessed into the back on the cabin trunk, with the lubber line on the aft end of the compass, giving a good line of vision from the helm. Extra lubber lines set at 45° are sometimes added to make the compass easier to read when the boat is heeling.

BOTTOM LEFT: Although fitted with an angular lubber line to make it easier to read from above, this compass is too close to the helm and doesn't follow the natural line of vision of the helmsman.

TOP RIGHT: The elaborate set-up on this old Norwegian rescue boat ensures the compass is completely protected from the elements. It can be read from the cockpit through the porthole and is lit up at night by the paraffin lamp.

BOTTOM RIGHT: This vintage compass is set into a table on the aft deck of the 1910 classic yacht Eveline. Only four cardinal points are shown, which makes reading of the intermediate points (eg NNW) extremely difficult – unlike the extremely detailed card of the Wilfred O White compass opposite.

BINNACLES

A binnacle is really just a fancy word for a compass stand. There are, however, certain important characteristics which this particular stand must fulfil. Crucially, it must not contain any ferrous metals which will exert a magnetic attraction ('deviation') on the compass – which is why most are made of wood, brass and, latterly, fibreglass or carbon fibre. Traditionally, a gimbal was fitted to keep the compass horizontal when the ship heeled over. And, from the 1880s onwards, many binnacles incorporated a pair of magnetic spheres (known as 'Kelvin's balls' after their inventor Lord William Kelvin) which could be adjusted to get rid of any deviation caused by the vessel's structure – especially on steel ships.

On modern yachts, the binnacle is usually incorporated into the wheel pedestal, along with repeaters for instruments such as the depth sounder, log and wind system. Gimbals aren't needed because modern spherical compasses aren't affected by boat heel. And, with minimal use of ferrous metals (apart from engines), Kelvin's balls have long been consigned to the nearest maritime museum.

OPPOSITE PAGE, CLOCKWISE FROM TOP LEFT: This fancy arrangement on the Dutch ocean racer Zwerver is possible because brass is non-magnetic, and therefore doesn't affect the compass. This binnacle is on a much bigger boat so it doesn't need a cowl to protect the compass from spray – just a bar to protect it from flying objects.
New and old combine with a brass binnacle and digital navigation display.
A spectacular brass binnacle with a pair of Kelvin's balls, worthy of the replica Herreshoff schooner Eleonora.
The modern equivalent is less spectacular – but possibly more accurate.
Another traditional-looking set-up on a replica classic yacht, also featuring Kelvin's balls.

BELOW: Compasses on modern yachts are usually fitted to the wheel pedestal, along with a digital navigation display. This entire arrangement is repeated on the other side of the yacht, for use when sailing on the other tack.

NAVIGATION LIGHTS

Ever since international rules were agreed in 1897, ships have been obliged by law to show lights while navigating at night. The application of these rules among yachts was somewhat lackadaisical, however, until the publication of the International Regulations for Prevention of Collisions at Sea (otherwise known as ColRegs) in 1972. This convention laid out a clear set of 'rules of the road' for vessels of all sizes, including stringent requirements for navigation lights. It included the description of lights to be shown in a variety of situations, from towing to fishing, running aground, or when a ship is generally restricted in its ability to manoeuvre (eg because it is dredging, or clearing mines).

Most yachts only need worry with the standard set of lights: Port (red), starboard (green) and stern (white) while sailing, plus a steaming light (white) while motoring. Boats under 65ft (20m) can get away with a combined tri-colour light at the top of the mast. And boats under 22ft (7m) need only shine a torch on their sail.

1. At night, all you would see of this yacht would be that small red (port) light on the bow. In any case, she has right of way because she is on starboard tack (ie the wind is coming from the starboard side).
2. A traditional bronze port light in a varnished wooden box – though the current recommendation is for the box to be painted black to show the light better.
3. A discreet port light fitted to the bulwark of a Greek day boat.
4. A bronze guard stops the glass getting smashed on this long-distance cruising yacht.

5. Yachts are obliged to show a single white light while at anchor overnight. Here, the traditional paraffin lantern has been replaced by a battery-operated alternative.
6. An old-fashioned brass stern lamp (white) has been fitted with an electric bulb on this 1959 classic yacht.
7. Another traditional port light in a wooden box which should be painted black.
8. A modern stern light fitted to the stern rail ('pushpit') of a production cruising yacht.

SOLAR & WIND POWER

OPPOSITE, TOP LEFT: A marine-grade turbine, such as this Air Breeze, is needed to cope with the corrosive effects of a sailing environment. Typically, these generators charge 12v or 24v batteries via a built-in regulator. At the helm are Jeremy and Fiona Rogers, builders of the legendary Contessa 32.

TOP RIGHT: Wind and sun power are being generated on this long-distance Norwegian cruising yacht spotted on Loch Ness in Scotland. Studies show that the wind blows strongly enough to make a significant charge less than 25% of the time, so it pays to have both systems.

BOTTOM: Happy times sailing out of Hobart, Tasmania, on a home-built wooden boat. These flexible solar panels give enough power for basic needs, such as lighting and starting the engine, but nowhere near enough to run a fridge or a modern telecommunication system.

THIS PAGE: There's a lot to be said for fitting your wind turbine high in the rigging, where it will make the most of any breeze and not cause any injury.

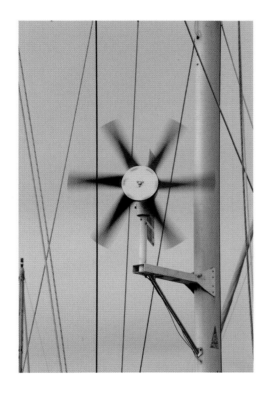

It's ironic that a sport which prides itself on harnessing nature can simultaneously do so much to harm it. For while most sailors are all too aware of the power of the wind while they are out sailing, once back at anchor most of them still invariably turn on their generators to power their fridges and laptops. Happily, renewable energy has come on in leaps and bounds in recent years, however, and more and more yachts are now being fitted with wind generators and solar panels. Partly this is because the cost of these appliances has gone down as the technology has advanced, and partly it's because of the proliferation of electronic and electrical equipment aboard most yachts. Even modest cruising boats are now fitted with GPS, chartplotters and fridges virtually as standard.

For the increasing band of converts, the big debate is whether to go for wind or solar power, and both have pros and cons. The main thing in favour of solar is that there are no moving parts and therefore less maintenance and repair issues, whereas advocates of wind power point out that, by definition, sailboats tend to be where the wind is. As prices of these machines tumble, the best solution for most yachts is to fit both. Either that, or get rid of the fridge.

GLOSSARY

For other terms, please refer to the relevant spread (see Contents page).

aft – At the back end of the boat

amidships – In the middle of the boat

backstay – The rigging that runs from the top of the mast to the back of the boat

ballast – Weight placed in the lowest part of the boat (usually the keel) to increase its stability

barque – A three-masted ship, with square sails on the two front masts and fore-and-aft sails on the back mast

battens – A thin strip of wood or other materials which slides into a pocket in the sail and helps flatten its trailing edge (or 'leech')

bawley – A type of traditional working boat native to the East Coast of Britain

beam – The width of a boat at its widest point

belaying pin – A short length of wood or metal which fits into a hole in a rail to form a cleat

bermudan – A triangular mainsail whose front edge is attached to the mast

boltrope – Rope stitched along the edge of a sail

bottlescrew – A threaded device at the bottom of the rigging used to tension the rig

bow – The front, or 'pointy' end, of a boat (though note that some boats can be 'pointy' at both ends!)

bulb keel – A fin keel with a lozenge-shaped weight at the bottom

bulkhead – A transverse 'wall' in the interior of a boat

carvel – A method of wooden hull construction using planks of wood fastened edge to edge

centreboard – A retractable keel

chainplate – A fitting used to attach standing rigging to the hull or deck

clew – Lower back corner of a sail

clinker – A method of wooden boatbuilding in which the lower edge of each plank overlaps the upper edge of the plank below it

coachroof – The top of the cabin

coaming – a) The raised edge of a cockpit which gives extra shelter; b) The timber fitted around a hole in the deck which forms the base of a hatch

compass rose – The circular illustration in a compass or on a chart which shows the compass gradations

counter – The back part of a boat which overhangs the water

cringle – A reinforced grommet in a sail

cunningham – A type of downhall (see below)

curragh – A traditional Irish working boat, built of canvas or leather stretched over a wooden frame

cutter – A sailboat with a single mast and at least two sails in front of the mast

danbuoy – A buoy with a tall pole and flag, used to indicate the position of an object - especially a man overboard

depth sounder – An electronic instrument used to measure the depth of the water

displacement – The weight of a boat, as measured by the weight of water it displaces when floating

downhaul – A pulley system used to tension the front edge of a sail

downwind – In the direction the wind is blowing towards

draft – The depth of a boat at its deepest point

ensign – A flag flown at the back of a vessel to denote its country of registration

fid – A short length of wood or metal used to lock a bowsprit or topmast in place

fiddles – A narrow strip of wood or other material attached to the edges of a table or other surface to prevent things sliding off

fin keel – A thin, narrow keel attached to the bottom of a yacht

foot – The bottom edge of a sail

fore-and-aft sail – A sail whose front edge is attached to the mast and which is set in a fore and aft direction

foresails – Sails set in front of the mast(s)

forestay – The rigging that runs from top of the mast (or part of the way up it) to the front of the boat

forward – Towards the front of the boat

freeboard – The vertical distance between the top edge of the hull and the sea

gaff sail – A four-sided sail which is hoisted up the mast on an angled spar (or 'gaff') which does not overlap the mast

galley – A ship's kitchen

genoa - A large sail set forward of the mast, which overlaps the mainsail

gimbals – A pivot arrangement allowing an item (such as a compass or stove) to remain level as the boat rolls

grating – A wooden grill used to cover a gangplank or the cockpit sole

gypsy – A pulley with a shaped groove that grips the links of a chain – usually fitted to an anchor windlass

halyard – Rope used to pull sails up the mast

head – Top corner of a bermudan (ie triangular) sail, or top edge of a four-sided sail

heads – A ship's toilet

jib – A small triangular sail set forward of the mast

junk – An Asian rig with square, fully-battened sails

keel – The longitudinal part of the hull that sticks out underneath

keelson – A longitudinal timber on a wooden boat which ties the transverse timbers (or 'floors') to the keel

ketch – A two-masted sailboat whose back mast is shorter than the front mast and is positioned in front of the helm

knot – A unit of measure for the speed of a boat, equivalent to 115mph

laid deck – A deck where individual planks of wood are laid onto deckbeams or a sub-deck

lanyard – A short length of line

lateen sail – A triangular sail set at an angle on a long spar which overlaps the mast

lazarette – A stowage area in the back of a boat

lead line – A method of measuring the depth of the sea using a lump of metal attached to a long line

lee cloth – A piece of canvas rigged to the side of a bunk to prevent the crew falling out

leech – The trailing edge of a sail

leeward – The direction or side of the boat away from the wind

log – A mechanical device, often a paddlewheel or propeller, used to measure the distance travelled though the water

long keel – A keel which runs the full length, or most of the length, of the boat

lubber line – A line on a compass used to read the vessel's course

luff – Front edge of a sail

lug sail – A four-sided sail set at an angle on a spar which overlaps the mast

mainsail – A large sail set behind and attached to the mast (the biggest mast, if more than one)

mainsheet – A line used to control the bottom, lower corner (or 'clew') of the mainsail

outhaul – A small line used to pull the corner of a sail to the end of a spar

overhangs – The parts of a boat at the front and back which extend over the water beyond the waterline

parrel beads – Wooden hoops strung on a line to prevent the line chafing the mast

peak – (noun) The upper, outermost corner of a gaff sail; (verb) To raise the upper, outermost corner of a gaff sail

pennants – Lines used to pull the aft corner of the sail to the boom when reefing

plum stem – A vertical bow

port – The side of a boat on the left when facing forward

pulpit – The fixed railing at the front of a boat

pushpit – The fixed railing at the back of a boat

rake – Angle at which a mast is inclined from the vertical – usually backwards

reef – To temporarily reduce the size of a sail, usually due to excessive wind

reefing points – A line of eyelets in a sail, fitted with lanyards to secure the sail when reefed

saildrive – A propulsion method where the propeller is driven through a leg protruding from the bottom of the hull

schooner – A sailboat with at least two masts of equal height, or whose back mast is the taller/tallest

scupper – A opening in the bulwarks or the sides of a hatch or vent, which allows the water to flow out

self-tailing – When the tail end of line doesn't need someone to hold it

sheave – A grooved wheel which a rope runs over, usually inside a block or mast

sheet – Line used to control the outer, lower corner of a sail

shroud – The rigging that gives lateral (ie sideways) support to the mast

skeg – An appendage immediately forward of the rudder that helps support and protect it

skylight – A large port with hinged windows mounted on the cabin top or deck

sloop – A sailboat with one mast, setting only one sail forward of the mast

smack – A type of traditional working boat native to the East Coast of Britain

spade rudder – A freestanding rudder not attached to a keel or skeg

spars – Collective term for masts, booms, gaffs, spinnaker poles, and so on

spinnaker – A large, balloon-like sail set forward of the mast

spoon bow – A bow with a rounded stem

sprayhood – A canvas shelter at the forward end of the cockpit to protect the crew from spray

square sails – Sails which hang from yards which are perpendicular to the hull

stanchion – An upright post that supports the guardrails around the outside of a boat

starboard – The side of a boat on the right when facing forward

stays – The rigging that supports the mast from the front and back on the boat

stem – The foremost part of the hull that rises up from the front end of the keel

stitch & glue – A boatbuilding method which involves stitching plywood planks together with wire and then gluing them in place

stock – The crossbar of an anchor

strip plank – A boatbuilding method which involves gluing narrow strips of wood together, edge to edge

tacking – Sailing at an angle of less than 90° to the wind, making progress to windward

toe rails – A low lip around the outside of a boat which helps to prevent people and objects rolling overboard

topping lift – A line from the top of the mast to the end of the boom that supports the boom when the sail is lowered

topsides – The part of the hull above the waterline

transom – The flat (usually back) end of a boat

traveller – A metal hoop which a sail is attached to and hoisted up or along a spar

turk's head – A type of decorative knot

upwind – In the direction the wind is coming from

waterline – The line on a boat's hull which the water reaches when it is normally laden

wetted surface – The area of a boat which is underwater

whipping – A covering of thin line wrapped around a line or other object to protect it

whipstaff – A primitive type of rudder

windjammer – Any large sailing vessel

windlass – Mechanical or electrical device used to recover the anchor and anchor chain

windward - In the direction the wind is coming from

yard – A horizontal spar which crosses the mast to which a sail is attached

yawl – A two-masted sailboat whose back mast is shorter than the front mast and is positioned behind the helm

INDEX

ACKNOWLEDGEMENTS

Many thanks to everyone at Adlard Coles, especially Elizabeth Multon,
for seeing this idea through – despite its traumatic birthing pains!
Thanks to Louise Turpin for her intuitive design work, and to Anna
for her sharp eyes.

All photos by Nic Compton, except:
Christian Février / Bluegreen: p24–25
Joe McCarthy: p161 (middle left); p162 (bottom left & bottom right);
p164 (top); p166 (top); p167 (bottom right); p168 (top left); p172 (top right)

Lines drawings by Will Stirling: p8–9, p24–25, p48–49, p108–109,
p120–121, p158–159 & p192
Lines drawings by Iain Oughtred: p170–171

*Answer to the puzzle on p47: Which boat does the unidentified William Fife
dragon belong to? It's the 1897 Cork One-Design* Jap.

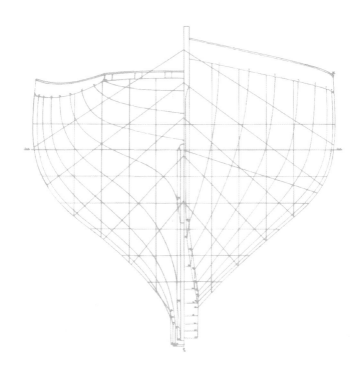